"Mark Hamilton has written a readable, accurate, biblically-based guide to ethics. He firmly but winsomely guides the uninitiated reader through the various debates about how to approach God's law as an ethical standard, helping the student to see the differences between legalism, theonomy, and antinomianism. He draws on a variety of Christian apologists—Van Til, Schaeffer, Lewis, Bahnsen, Sire, and Pink—but never overwhelms the reader. The last chapter makes the ethics students apply what has gone before by urging them to test the morality of their contemplated actions against the requirements of the Scriptures. Clear, concise, and helpful!"

–**Dr. John A. Sparks**, Retired Dean of Arts & Letters and Professor of Law. Grove City College, Grove City, PA.

"When I was in college in the 70s books like *A Primer on Biblical Ethics* were commonly read by Christian students. We truly wanted to know how to respond to the moral upheaval of the sexual revolution and the confusion which was America at the time. Today, Mark Hamilton has met a need for college students who also are facing a country that has lost its moral and ethical compass. Not only will they learn about ethics but they will learn about the greatness of their God and Father of our Lord Jesus Christ. This book is sobering and I hope students today will read it and heed its great truths!"

–**Joe Maggelet**, Navigators and FCA Staff, Ashland University. Grace Brethren Elder/Pastor, Ashland, OH.

"I highly recommend *A Primer On Biblical Ethics* to anyone wanting to know about living a civil life. Mark Hamilton takes his expertise as a university professor and gives the correct analysis to the various origins of law and contextualizes ethics. He does an excellent job using the foundation of Holy Scripture as the place to start. I have read many works on ethics and I can tell you this is the book you should read because the others will pale in comparison. Mark's most excellent work will give you a complete volume. If you are a young person ready for life or marriage this can serve as a premarital handbook! It will be an investment into your life you will not regret."

–**Mark Stevenson**, Director, Ohioans for Educational Freedom, published author and minister, Husband and Father of four.

D1563959

"Contemporary Christianity may be dubbed lawless for the fact that so few know or understand the Ten Commandments, which is the core and substance of Biblical Ethics. Dr. Hamilton's book is timely in that it provides a way for Christians to be Christian again."

–**Matthew Timmons**, Elder/Pastor of Providence Church, Ashland, OH, ordained pastor in the Presbyterian Church in America (PCA).

"There was a time in my life when loving God was a 'heart' and 'might' effort. I had little understanding of what it meant to love Him with my mind. Trying to do this, looking over the disorganized pile of Christian information about ethics, confessions, creeds, doctrines and philosophies made my theology look like an upturned box of Legos®. Mark Hamilton helped organize these essential building blocks in my mind in much the same way he has done in this *A Primer On Biblical Ethics*. This book was for me a reminder of the need for good teachers and clear material to make sense of it all. Well done!"

–**Mark Robinette** is pastor of Foundation Church in Mt. Sterling, Ohio, the director of development for the Slavic Reformation Society, founder of the missions' organization Mission to Myanmar and Chairman of the Board for Reformation Theological Seminary in Yangon.

"This is a clear and easy read that nails the basics of ethics in a straightforward sweep. My compliments to Professor Hamilton!"

–**Nathanael Mark Robinette**, well-read Tenth-Grade Homeschooler.

A Primer On Biblical Ethics

Mark J. Hamilton

Pilgrim Platform
Marietta, Ohio

Copyright ©2014 Mark Hamilton
All rights reserved.

ISBN: 978-0-9839046-8-7
Edition: 2014.8.15

Published by

Pilgrim Platform
149 E. Spring St., Marietta
Ohio, 45750
www.pilgrim-platform.org

Biblical quotations are from the *New American Standard Version*,
The Locman Foundation, 1995, unless otherwise cited.

Printed in the United States of America

To Alex and Jaime Searls

*On November 2, 2007 seventeen-year-old
Alex Searls of Zanesville, Ohio, was
tragically killed in an accident. His mother,
Jaime, made the gracious decision to donate
his organs for transplantation. The next
morning I was the privileged beneficiary of
Alex's liver. Without this heartbreak and a
mother's compassionate action I would not be
alive to write this book.
I humbly thank Jamie Searls.*

TABLE OF CONTENTS

ACKNOWLEDGMENTS

I thank God for His mercy and grace that has rescued me from sin and sustained me through this writing project. Thanks to my parents Bob and Grace Hamilton who exposed me to the Gospel when I was quite young. I thank my dear wife, Pat, for her constant love even when I am not so lovable and for her great perseverance in helping to keep me alive; and my daughters and sons-in-law Tess and Brandon Kubitz, Kristen and Anthony Tobias and their children Grace and Xander who fill my life with great joy.

Thank you to Ashland University for supporting me with a Sabbatical for the 2012 Fall Semester when I was able to transcribe many class lecture notes into this manuscript. Thanks to all my many students at Ashland University who have read various drafts of this text, have provided me valuable feedback and who keep me eager to continue in the classroom. Thank you to Matt Timmons, Craig Redmond, Joe Maggelet, Dave Lillo, Jim Deweese, and Eric Wagner who read early manuscripts and offered valuable comments. Thanks to my dear friends at Providence Church who demonstrate to me what obedience to the Gospel means and thanks to Phillip Ross, my publisher at Pilgrim-Platform.

PREFACE

In the Old Testament book of Ecclesiastes Solomon concludes that there is nothing new under the sun. Of course he was mistaken because automobiles, airplanes, televisions and computers had not been invented and they would certainly be new. Solomon, however, was not speaking about novel technological developments but rather about how the world is and how humans behave. In these there has been no change. Though moral values may change from culture to culture, humans behave as they always have demonstrating works of great honor and dignity yet doing the most heinous actions imaginable. This text provides nothing new about human nature and human behavior. Nor does it provide any new solutions to the problems created by immoral human actions. No new insight will be provided that hasn't already been uttered. If you find something new then please inform me and I'll have it removed before any more are printed. There are no new ideas in it and certainly no new ideas about Christian ethics. Then why write it?

Humans have feeble memories and the memory of Christian values has rapidly waned in the last couple of generations so there is a great need to remind people what Christianity is. A few years ago, I heard James Sire, then the editor for InterVarsity Press; make comment that he tells college students that they cannot reject Christianity. He adds that they cannot reject it because they don't know it well enough to reject it. Since then, I have often expressed that same thought. Most college students today have a minimum of accurate knowledge of the Bible or what Christianity is all about; they understand even less about Christian ethics. It is important to clarify what a Christian ethic should look like because there are so few exceptional examples of lived out Biblical Christianity. Most people have only a vague understanding of what Christian morality should look like. This book has as its educational purpose to bring to remembrance accurate knowledge of Christianity and of Christian ethics. It is specifically directed to those who may think they have an understanding of Christianity because they have an acquaintance with it, but who are generally quite ignorant.

A second reason for its writing is that old truths need to be repackaged so that they remain understandable and relevant to each new generation. So while there is nothing new here, I pray it will be said in ways that communicate to a new generation. These values first communicated in the ancient world need to be restated in ways that our society, the church, and current students can grasp and apply. This work attempts to whittle down the essence of Christian ethics into a read-able and usable contemporary summary.

1. Introduction

With the increasing influences of postmodernism, relativism, and the lack of a cultural center there has been little to prevent Western society from entering into moral chaos. The memory of Christian values has eroded from much of the West. Once it was commonly believed that right and wrong must be determined by an objective absolute standard understood as God, but this is no longer the case. Traditional values have long since disappeared along with any Christian consensus. Establishing moral values no longer depends on a transcendent authority but ethics are now created by humans for power purposes. Humans have become the final arbiters of values and these standards are subjectively[1] chosen; all that remains are practical tenets created by humans for their own independent pragmatic reasons. The attempt to establish human-centered

---

1 *Subjectively* means personally or individually.

theories of ethics has led us only to skepticism about morality and relativism in human practice.

A generation ago Francis Schaeffer noted that Western Civilization had exhausted all of its attempts to develop a comprehensive world view in a rational way, beginning from human experience and from naturalistic assumptions. He observed that this led to the conclusion to either give up the quest for a metaphysical explanation of the universe, surrender reason embracing irrationalism (which has certainly happened in the West in existentialism and then postmodernism), or find a new starting point for metaphysics and ethics.[2] Many have abandoned the quest for a unified metaphysic or for universal values reducing philosophy to the two options of the study of language and logic, or have gone the route of irrationality becoming existentialists or postmoderns. The alternative proposal endorsed here is that the sole way to maintain rationality and an ethic with universal values and absolutes is to begin with a different starting point. Rather than beginning with autonomous[3] humanistic assumptions, we must begin with the stated belief that God exists and that He has communicated truth in Scripture. This project sets forth a non-

2 Francis Schaeffer clearly articulated this need in the 1970's in his books, *The God Who is There*, and *How Shall We Then Live*.

3 *Autonomous* means free or without restraint.

sectarian Christian moral framework, one that could be described as Biblical and Protestant from the essential presupposition that God exists, is good, and communicates His moral nature to His creation most specifically through the Bible. It is also theological since theology is foundational to all areas of study.

Because life has universal ethical dimensions to it there has obviously been a multitude of Christian writings on ethics. There is also much agreement among Christian ethicists, though numerous differences in focus and emphasis certainly exist. One might even divide these traditional systems into four schools: Liberal, Roman Catholic, Anabaptist, and Reformed. All (except the Liberal which would make reason equal to or superior to scripture) would claim to be essentially biblical in some way, so they would all claim to be called Biblical Ethics though they would not mean the same thing by this claim. The general hermeneutical[4] difference in these three traditions is that the Roman Catholic would emphasize tradition and reason as sharing authority or having equal authority with Scripture, the Anabaptist focuses almost exclusively on New Testament moral teaching particularly as found in the gospels or sayings of Jesus (especially the

---

4   *Hermeneutics* in theology is the theory of biblical inter-
    pretation.

Sermon on the Mount), while the Reformed tradition emphasizes the continuity of morality as found in the entirety of Scripture both Old and New Testaments. Reformed hermeneutics also begins with the assumption that Scripture interprets Scripture, meaning that any individual passage of the Bible can best be understood in the context and the light of the totality of the Bible.

Making moral decisions necessitates a guiding standard. "Every one of us needs a moral compass to guide us through the maze of moral issues and disagreements that confront us every moment of our lives."[5] Regardless of Christian denomination the one standard found among them should be that the Bible is the primary source of knowledge about what is right and wrong, and its books are inspired by God.

> "**All Scripture** is given by inspiration of God, and is profitable for doctrine, for reproof, for correction, for instruction in righteousness: that the man of God may be perfect, thoroughly furnished for all good works" (2 Timothy 3:16).

The distinctive nature of this work is that it is explicitly Biblical and embraces the entirety of Scripture. Biblical ethics is the philosophy of life which the Bible entails, and the Christian faith of

---

5   Greg Bahnsen, *By This Standard*, (Tyler, TX: The Institute for Christian Economics, 1985), 14.

the Bible yields. The *Westminster Confession of Faith* states,

> "The authority of the Holy Scripture, for which
> it ought to be believed, and obeyed depends
> not upon the testimony of any man, or Church;
> but wholly upon God (who is truth itself) the
> author thereof and therefore it is to be received,
> because it is the Word of God" (1:4).[6]

---

6   The *Westminster Confession*, written by a gathering of
    Christian scholars in England in the 1640s, is the confes-
    sional statement of belief for Presbyterian denomina-
    tions, Reformed Churches, and the Puritans. It is a bril-
    liant, lucid document explaining Christian doctrine and
    Church polity.

2. THE FOUNDATION FOR BIBLICAL ETHICS

Most theories of morality other than the nineteenth and twentieth century irrationalists traditionally have a high view of human reason and are optimistic that the combination of reason and science can determine right and wrong. The Christian ethical system, however, does not begin with human reason creating a list of arbitrary do's and don'ts, rather it grows out of the person and character of God Himself. The starting presupposition for Christian ethics is very different from theories which begin with humanity's autonomous reason attempting to figure out the universe and to discover the ethical structure in that universe through the efforts of human reason. Christian ethics does not start with humans, like other systems do; Christian ethics is theocentric, meaning God-centered.

What is meant by the concept God? The Biblical approach begins with the assumption that God exists[1] and this God is not a vague entity, nor vacuous, nor silent about Himself and the world He has made. Certain very specific things can be said about the Christian's God because He has not left humans in darkness but has revealed certain information about Himself to enlighten the human race. God reveals knowledge of Himself, including knowledge of certain attributes which describe His nature, most importantly His moral essence. These attributes are foundational for ethics.

Divine Attributes as Foundational

Arthur Pink states, "The foundation of all true knowledge of God must be a clear mental apprehension of His perfections as revealed in Holy Scripture. An unknown God can neither be trusted, served, nor worshipped."[2] God has certain descriptive qualities frequently called attributes. These attributes are important and inseparable from one another, and specific ones have particular relevance to the development and discussion of ethics. God is **infinite** referring to His unlimited nature. God is not limited by space

---

1   The first book of the Bible is Genesis and it begins, "In the beginning God created the heavens and the earth."

2   Arthur Pink, *The Attributes of God*, (Grand Rapids: Baker Books, 1975), 7.

(immensity) or time (eternity) but is beyond both. 1 Kings 8:27 declares, "God is the everlasting God." Revelation 1:8 proclaims, "I am the Alpha and the Omega," says the Lord God, "who was, and who is, and who is to come, the Almighty." As such He is without beginning or end. God is the **creator** over all that exists. This is directly related to **God's transcendence,** and refers to God being beyond the universe, being outside of the universe and unable to be fundamentally changed by forces found in the universe. The universe is not God, and is not an extension of God's being as is taught in pantheistic or panentheistic traditions.[3] God is not identical with any of the stuff of the universe. God creates the universe outside of His own being and not as an extension of His being. To call God transcendent means that God is above all that exists and is the creator of all that is not His Being. In ethics this allows for the theoretical possibility for evil to exist in the created world and for God to be untainted by it in His uncreated being. This is the claim of Christianity: that God can remain perfectly good and holy while

---

3   *Pantheistic* and *panentheistic* religious belief systems are primarily founded on eastern philosophical traditions that believe the universe is God or an extension of God's being. As such the universe and God have no ontological distinction from one another. The universe "flows" or emanates from God. It is not God's creation.

real evil exists in the world, because God is transcendent and separate in essence from the evil found in fallen creation.

God is **almighty** and rules over everything that He has made. God is the **sovereign** king of the universe; nothing happens outside of God's control. **Providence** asserts that God brings all things to their completed purpose. God is **omnipresent**, meaning present everywhere. No one can flee from a God who is **immanent** (near) or present everywhere at all times. The Psalmist writes, "If I ascend to heaven, Thou art there: If I make my bed in Sheol,[4] behold, Thou art there" (Psalm 139:8). God is not the "material stuff" of the universe, but His presence is everywhere in the universe and beyond.

In Acts 17 the apostle Paul enters Athens and encounters the Greek philosophers. Paul observes them worshiping a statue with the inscription, "To the unknown God." He declares to them that the God who made heaven and earth does not live in objects built by human hands. A transcendent God is not part of the world He made, so He cannot dwell in humanly constructed shrines. But then Paul adds nevertheless as your own (Greek) poets have written, "In Him we live and have our being." God is near, close at hand, or immanent. This combination of a God who is

---

4   Sheol is the place of the dead.

both transcendent and immanent is unique to
Christianity. God is present everywhere, but is
distinct from the substance of the universe. This
makes it quite difficult to reconcile the Christian
idea of God to the idea of God found in other
religious traditions which understand God to be
primarily or exclusively either transcendent and
unreachable or immanent and part of nature
itself.

Omnipotence refers to God as all-powerful.
Some mistakenly think this means that God can
do anything. It does not. God has one limitation
and that limitation is His own nature. God's
character is a unity; His attributes are inseparable
from one another. God cannot deny Himself,
says 2 Timothy 2:13. God cannot become less
than God, so He cannot violate any of His other
attributes. By denying any one of His other
attributes then God would be less than God,
which would be the one thing God is incapable
of becoming. In other words, God can do anything consistent with His own nature, consistent
to who He is. God cannot violate Himself; God
cannot *not* be God. Therefore, omnipotence
means that nothing outside of God's own being
can limit God. There are no principles of truth,
goodness, or beauty that are next to or above
God according to which He has patterned the

world.[5] Since God is **good**, He cannot become less than good, so He cannot do or be evil. If God is the source for **rationality** then God cannot do the irrational; He cannot make a square circle or a round square, for these are self-contradictory and irrational and for God to do the irrational would be for God to deny Himself. God can do the physically impossible but not the logically or intrinsically impossible. In *The Problem of Pain*, C.S Lewis states,

> "His Omnipotence means power to do all that is intrinsically possible, not to do the intrinsically impossible. You may attribute miracles to him, but not nonsense. This is no limit to his power."[6]

God is **personal**, denoting He is self-conscious and self-willing; God thinks and acts as a self.

> "Personality requires two basic characteristics: (1) self-reflection and (2) self-determination …. God is personal in that he knows himself to be and he possesses the characteristics of self-determination."[7]

---

5   Cornelius Van Til, *The Defense of the Faith*, (Philadelphia: The Presbyterian and Reformed Publishing Company, 1955), 12.

6   C. S. Lewis, *The Problem of Pain*, (New York: Harper-Collins, 1996), 18.

7   James Sire, *The Universe Next Door*, (Downers Grove, Illinois: InterVarsity Press, 1976), 26.

God is not a cosmic blob or impersonal energy, though He is a living God with energy. Being personal does not mean that God is a human being, though it does not negate the possibility of His becoming one if so willed (the example of Jesus Christ). God is complete, absolute personality with acute self-awareness. As personal it is quite appropriate to describe God with a personal pronoun (He). God is not an impersonal "It." This is foundational if God is going to have the ability to communicate to other persons (humans or rational beings), particularly about His moral character, and expect them to follow suit with moral actions.

God is **triune or is a Trinity**. This is a doctrine unique to Christian theology and distinguishes Christianity from other Western religious traditions such as Islam and Judaism, which emphasize the unity and indivisibility of God. In Christianity God is one Being in three Persons. God's oneness cannot be separated from His threeness and His threeness cannot be separated from His oneness. They are both essential to God's nature and are equally ultimate in God's very being. In philosophical language God has unity and plurality, oneness and manyness, in His nature. The Trinity also presents a solution to the historic philosophical problem of the One and the Many.[8] The most succinct statement on the Trinity was formulated in the fourth century in the Athanasian Creed. A section of it states,

"That we worship one God in Trinity, and Trinity in Unity; Neither confounding the persons nor dividing the substances. For there is one person of the Father, another of the Son, and another of the Holy Spirit. But the God-head of the Father, of the Son, and of the Holy Spirit is all one, the glory equal, the majesty co-eternal. Such as the Father is, such is the Son, and such is the Holy Spirit. The Father uncre-ated, the Son uncreated, and the Holy Spirit uncreated. The Father incomprehensible, the Son incomprehensible, and the Holy Spirit in-comprehensible. The Father eternal, the Son eternal, and the Holy Spirit eternal. And yet there are not three uncreated nor three incom-prehensible, but one uncreated and one incom-prehensible. So likewise the Father is almighty, the Son is almighty, the Holy Spirit is almighty. And yet they are not three almighties but one almighty. So the Father is God, the Son is God, and the Holy Spirit is God; And yet they are not three Gods, but one God. So likewise the Father is Lord, the Son is Lord, and the Holy Spirit is Lord; And yet they are not three Lords but one Lord …. And in this Trinity none is

---

8   A well formulated discussion on the philosophical One and Many problem from a Christian perspective explaining how the doctrine of the Trinity resolves this issue is found in Rousas Rushdoony's book, *The One and The Many*.

afore or after another; none is greater or less than another. But the whole three persons are coeternal and coequal. So that in all things, as aforesaid, the Unity in Trinity and the Trinity in Unity is to be worshiped.

THE MORAL ATTRIBUTES OF GOD

God has unchanging moral attributes which can analogously be transferred to finite human beings. The most important and general of these attributes is God's goodness; **God is good**. This is also called God's omnibenevolence. There is no higher good than God, nor is anything truly good apart from God. In the *Euthyphro* (written by Plato) Socrates asks Euthyphro whether the gods love piety because it is pious or whether it is pious because the gods love it.[9] Socrates is actually asking Euthyphro whether the virtues are higher "in being" or by nature (ontologically) than the gods or vice versa, that the gods are the source of the virtues. Does God have to attain the good in order to become good, or is God the creator and source of all goodness? The Greek gods were finite and often quite despicable so they were in need of a transcendent good higher than themselves. If good and evil are categories independent of God, then God cannot be the source of morality. This is important because

9   Plato, "Euthyphro," in *The Trial and Death of Socrates*, (Indianapolis: Hackett Publishing Co., 2000), 11.

Greek ideas of the good were higher and greater than their finite gods.

In contrast, when speaking of the infinite Christian God there is no higher source of good than God; God is the highest good. God is the foundation, source, and essence of goodness. God cannot deny Himself so there is no evil or moral darkness in God; He cannot do evil, for that would be contradictory to God's good character. Some have challenged this Christian belief in God's absolute goodness by accusing it of being an arbitrary standard. It is not an arbitrary goodness because God's attributes are a unity and God's goodness is grounded in and inseparable from His eternal unchanging nature. **Immutability**[10] eliminates any arbitrariness or subjectivity to the standard of goodness. There are numerous other moral attributes that stem from God's goodness which include but are not limited to grace, righteousness, love, mercy, and justice. Holiness is another moral attribute. The absolute holiness of God is clearly emphasized throughout Scripture and refers to God being internally and eternally perfect. Holiness also refers to God's complete separation from sin and corruption, and is the only attribute elevated in Scripture to the third degree, as God is called

---

10 *Immutability* is the divine attribute of being unchange-
    able in nature.

"Holy, Holy, Holy."[11] It is separation from all imperfection and pure from any stain of sin.

> "God's holy character is back of his expressed requirement of man that he must be perfect as a creature. What God says is right is right because he says it and he says it because it rests on his holy nature."[12]

HUMANS CREATED IN THE IMAGE OF GOD

Psalm 8:4 asks, "What is man, that Thou dost take thought of him?" This is answered in Genesis 1:26-27 which reads,

> "Then God said, 'Let us make man in Our image, according to Our likeness; and let them rule over the fish of the sea and over the birds of the sky and over the cattle and over all the earth, and over every creeping thing that creeps on the earth.' God created man in His own image, in the image of God He created him; male and female He created them."

Christianity recognizes the uniqueness of all human beings created by God and designated by God to rule over all of creation. It also affirms

---

11 This implies God is holy, holier, and holiest. No other divine attribute in Scripture is elevated to the third degree. God is never called good, good, good, or almighty, almighty, almighty. This expresses the supreme importance of God's holiness.

12 Van Til, 11.

that male and female are both made in God's image.

Humans are created in the image of God meaning that humans share certain "god-like" qualities. This does not refer to any physical qualities. Neither are humans like God in terms of infinity or immutability. We are not omniscient or omnipotent; these are incommunicable[13] traits. Humans are personal, created with a personality, meaning self-conscious and self-determining, like God. God is omniscient or all knowing; whereas humans made in His image do not know everything, but are capable of having true finite knowledge. We are finite replicas of God and similar to Him in numerous ways. Because God and humans are both personal there is the possibility of interpersonal communication between the infinite personal and the finite personal, as the infinite personal communicates to human beings (the finite personal).

Being finite or lacking knowledge is never the immediate cause of human sin or immorality. As such, the Christian view of epistemology[14] is that the personal God communicates true knowledge about Himself, about the universe He has created, including knowledge about humans and

---

13 Incommunicable attributes are ones that are not transferable from God to one of His created beings.

14 *Epistemology* is the theory of knowledge or how we know what we know.

the nature of good and evil. Though humans do not have exhaustive knowledge about everything, accurate knowledge or truth can be known as God reveals it. "God is omniscient; His knowledge is not acquired, and His knowledge, according to common terminology, is intuitive while man's is discursive."[15] In other words, the Christian view of knowledge is that humans created in God's image have true knowledge when they think God's thoughts after Him, including moral knowledge of the good. This communication is called revelation. "Revelation is to be regarded as the disclosure to man on the part of God of his mind and will."[16] If the moral declarations by God in the Bible could not be known by human minds, then the idea of revealed moral knowledge would be meaningless.

Humans are gifted with rational, intellectual faculties and a creative capacity which gives the means of developing the sciences, philosophies, and arts. This is also the basis for our being moral agents with the capacity to distinguish good from evil. God desires humans to be Holy as He is Holy. In their original state humans are created holy, good, morally unflawed, and thus com-

15 Gordon Clark, "The Bible as Truth" in *The Trinity Review*, no. 280, (Unicoi, Tennessee: The Trinity Foundation, 2008), 3.
16 John Murray, *Principles of Conduct*, (Grand Rapids: Eerdmans Publishing, 1957), 8.

pletely obedient to God's perfect moral law.
Humans are endowed with a moral sensitivity
enabling them to differentiate between right and
wrong, to choose good and evil, and to concern
themselves with the welfare of other humans.
Our distinguishing characteristic is that we can
know God if we will seek Him and thus find the
way that we should walk. Our uniqueness lies in
the fact that humans alone are allied to the divine
by our nature.[17] Humans are uniquely created by
God in His image with intrinsic value and worth
from conception through death. This is the
philosophical basis for the inherent worth in
humans and this has pronounced consequences
for ethics. All humans have equal value because
they are each equally made in the image of God;
this is the basis for any appeal to human rights.

God Communicates His Moral Nature to Creation

Christian morality is grounded in an objective reality, a personal good God who exists. This
Deity communicates His moral nature to humans
created in His image. Because of this there are
values that are true for everyone for all time
founded on God's character. Christianity believes
there are moral absolutes. ***We are moral beings***

---

17 Levi Olan, "The Nature of Man," in *Great Jewish Ideas*,
     (Clinton, Massachusetts: The Colonial Press 1964), 167.

living in a moral universe created by a moral God. God's communication to humans is understood historically to be done through two means: general (natural) revelation and special (supernatural) revelation, which are both based on and reflective of the character of God.

NATURE AS GENERAL REVELATION

General revelation is the knowledge of God communicated universally and naturally available to all humans since they live in God's created world. General revelation is communicated through three means: nature, conscience, and providence. This belief that nature is the voice of God is founded on Psalm 19:1-4b which says,

> "The heavens are telling of the glory of God;
> And their expanse is declaring the work of His hands. Day to day pours forth speech, And night to night reveals knowledge. There is no speech, nor are their words; Their voice is not heard. Their line (sound) has gone out through all the earth, And their utterances to the end of the world."

There are also many passages such as Psalm 29 which speak of the majestic voice of God thundering over the waters. And even more importantly for ethics Romans 1:18-20 adds,

> "For the wrath of God is revealed from heaven against all ungodliness and unrighteousness of

> men, who suppress the truth in unrighteous-
> ness, because that which is known about God is
> evident within them; for God made it evident
> to them. For since the creation of the world His
> invisible attributes, His eternal power and di-
> vine nature, have been clearly seen, being un-
> derstood through what has been made, so that
> they are without excuse."

Nature points to the existence of the Creator and speaks of God's greatness and splendor. Nature shows humans that God is the Creator and that humans should bow before Him.

Conscience as General Revelation

Closely associated with natural revelation is the belief that God places an innate internal sense of right and wrong on the hearts of humans. Romans 2:14-15 unabashedly affirms this,

> "For when Gentiles[18] who do not have the law
> do instinctively the things of the law, these, not
> having the law are a law to themselves, in that
> they show the work of the law written in their
> hearts, their conscience bearing witness, and
> their thoughts alternately accusing or else de-
> fending them."

All humans have knowledge of God and of His law written on their hearts and known through this innate knowledge and the moral structure of

---

18 Gentiles are all non-Jews.

the world. Thus, no one can plead moral ignorance before God. The moral law written on the
human heart produces the conscience, but due to
the hardness of the human heart untrained conscience is often obscured by human sin, and as
such may be vague in those who ignore it.
Because of this, conscience performs more of a
function of judgment and condemnation than as
a tool for providing clear moral direction. It does
work to restrain evil, however, and for those who
listen to its voice, it can become quite refined;
and in those who ignore it the conscience can
become overly calloused and severed even leading to psychopathic disorders.

All humans have both an inward and outward
witness to God's existence. It is not a saving
knowledge to be sure, but as a condemning
knowledge natural revelation still provides
knowledge of God.[19] So although humans are
given an inherent sense of good and evil, in our
fallen context this cannot provide salvation, and
alone it cannot be our sole guide for ethics.

PROVIDENCE AND GENERAL REVELATION

Providence is the belief that God governs and
directs all the affairs of humans and is sovereign
over human history. As one observes God's direct

19 Greg Bahnsen, *Always Ready*, (Atlanta: American Vi-
    sion, 1996), 38.

leading of human affairs one sees the revealing of God. It is less directly related to ethics than conscience, but certainly a part of general revelation. God reveals knowledge of Himself through sovereign divine acts of governance in history. This is less confrontational than other means of revelation and less distinctively moral; this also makes providence psychologically easier to be denied.

NATURAL LAW

Natural law is the belief there is a moral order built into nature and understood by human reason. It is what is right by nature; and as a theory it existed prior to Christianity and is not dependent on the God of Christianity. Many non-Christians actually hold to a form of this when they express the belief that nature is moral and reason is able to extrapolate just standards from nature's ethical structure.[20] Natural law looks for a foundation for moral law internal to humans by appealing to a common rationality.[21] We find natural law affirmed in the American Declaration of Independence when it states that "we hold these truths to be self-evident that all men are created equal endowed by their creator with cer-

---

20 Among those considered to hold such a view of natural law are the Stoics and Aristotle.

21 Rousas Rushdoony, *The Institutes of Biblical Law*, (The Presbyterian and Reformed Publishing Co., The Craig Press, 1973), 685.

tain inalienable rights." This supports the belief that the light of human reason by itself is capable of grasping certain moral truths found in the external world. There is a strong tradition among Christians, especially Catholics (through Thomas Aquinas), who have adopted a form of natural law and believe that it is fundamental to ethics and law. This belief emphasizes the capacity of human reason to understand the moral structure found in some detail in nature

Determining specific ethical principles from nature through reason is highly speculative, however. In the revelation found in nature through general revelation there is enough knowledge for humans to reject God and His revelation; there is enough knowledge for condemnation but not enough for salvation, nor enough to create a detailed system of morality. Nature certainly bears witness to the reality of moral law, but there is not enough external information determined through such means to provide sufficient moral knowledge to know God's will with any in-depth detail or specificity. Nature provides enough knowledge to provide a standard by which humans can be judged.

Humans cannot escape general revelation. "All reality is revelational of God and cannot be truly understood apart from Him."[22] This leaves

---

22 Ibid., 684.

humans "without excuse" before God. "As sinners all men refuse to acknowledge their Creator and live by His revelation. Hence we can say that men both know and do not know God; they know Him in judgment."[23] There are theological difficulties with depending on natural law as the basis for a moral theory. Natural law relies very heavily upon human reason and upon the natural condition of the earth. This conflicts with the Biblical assertion that nature is significantly corrupted through the effects of the curses on nature after the fall from grace in the Garden of Eden. Genesis 3:17-18a says, "Cursed is the ground because of you; In toil you shall eat of it All the days of your life. Both thorns and thistles it shall grow for you." Nature has been altered as a consequence of human sin because humans, being in a position of dominion over creation, were mediators between God and nature, and as humans sinned there were damaging effects on nature. It can also be argued biblically that there is significant damage done to human reason by the effects of the fall on the first humans, and a subsequent effect on all successive generations. Ephesians 4:17-18 states,

> "This I say therefore, and affirm together with the Lord, that you walk no longer just as the Gentiles also walk, in the futility of their mind,

23 Bahnsen, *Always Ready*, 38.

being darkened in their understanding, ex-
cluded from the life of God, because of the ignorance that is in them, because of the hardness
of their heart."

Since nature has been cursed and damaged by
the effects of the fall and human reason has been
darkened by sin, the ability to decipher the moral
law correctly through nature is futile. There is
certainly a moral design placed in creation, but
after the Fall this design is obscured to sinful
human reason. Deriving morality from nature
creates a type of natural law that is so abstract and
vague that all sorts of "bad law" can appeal to it as
its source. For example, if one believes that natural selection is derived from observation of
nature, then it can be argued that the atrocities of
eugenics[24] based upon the survival of the fittest as
a foundation for morality could be induced from
observations of nature.

While the means provided by general revelation are legitimate sources of knowledge about
God, they are not sufficient enough to provide
extensive moral direction. In the current state of
affairs it is impossible to rely on reason's ability to
accurately understand the nature of a moral universe by our own fallen efforts. Humans need
something more explicit. "Because of the corrup-

---

24 *Eugenics* is the concept of selective breeding in humans
   to achieve improved genetic qualities.

tion of his powers by sin it is necessary that
mankind receives a definitive, objective, written
statement of the righteousness of God."[25]

---

25 William O. Einwechter, *Walking in the Law of the Lord,*
   (Hopeland, PA: Durash Press, 2010), 70.

3. God's Law

Special Revelation

Proverbs1:7 states, "The beginning of knowledge is fear of the Lord." The starting point for all knowledge is God's special revelation of Himself. Special revelation is the revealing or communicating of specific information by God to humans through supernatural means, most specifically through the Holy Scriptures. Nothing is truly known unless it is known in its proper relationship to God. The historical Christian view of epistemology[1] is based on the underlying belief that the Word of God is the ultimate reference point of knowledge, including moral knowledge. Hebrews 1:1-2 provides a rich statement summarizing God's communication through special revelation,

> "God, after He spoke long ago to the fathers in the prophets in many portions and in many

---

1 *Epistemology* is the theory of knowledge or how we know what we know.

ways, in these last days has spoken to us in His
Son, whom He appointed heir of all things
through whom also He made the world."

God reveals in the Scriptures detailed knowledge about Himself, about the means of salvation
through Christ, and about the world we live in,
including providing moral instruction. "The only
tenable approach to the laws operative over and
within the natural world is thus through the
supernatural law word of God."[2] All Scripture is
God's specially revealed law-word; the heart of
that law is the law of Moses[3] and the epitome of
God's special revelation is the person of Jesus
Christ. All we need to really know about right
and wrong is found in God's law-word. Jesus
regarded Scripture highly and claimed it to be
authoritative. In John 17:17 He declares God's
Word is truth and in John 10:35 that "Scripture
cannot be broken." God has spoken through
propositional revelation.[4] Concerning the truth
claims made in the Bible,

> "Let it be said that the truth of statements in the
> Bible is the same type of truth as is claimed for
> ordinary statements, such as: Columbus discov-
> ered America, two plus two are four, and a fall-

2 Rushdoony, 684.
3 Ibid., 675.
4 *Propositional revelation* is the belief that God communicates to humans in complete clear statements and
   thoughts.

ing body accelerates at thirty-two feet per second. So far as the meaning of truth is concerned the statement 'Christ died for our sins' is on the same level as any ordinary, everyday assertion that happens to be true."[5]

God's law-claims put forward in special revelation are propositional, verbal forms of revelation. This means the law is declarative and is stated in words and sentences in a logical sense. Because of this it can be known by the human mind as direct truth itself. God has spoken in words that are adequate symbols of the conceptual content that is literally true, and this is the point of coincidence between the knowledge of God and the knowledge received by humans.[6]

BIBLICAL LAW

Special revelation found in Scripture as God's law is the foundation and necessary standard for Christian ethics. In Biblical law God's moral character is expressed and communicated to humans in His image. "The law of God proceeds from and is based on God's own divine perfections. The moral law is the revelation of the moral attributes of God Himself in terms of what God wills for man."[7] The moral law found in

---

5 Gordon H. Clark, 1.

6 Ibid., 6.

7 Einwechter, 35.

Scripture is like God, and since God does not change, neither does His law.

The theory of ethics that God directly tells us what is true, what is right and wrong, what is good and evil for all spheres of human life, is generally referred to as the **Divine Command Theory** of ethics. One specific type of Divine Command Theory is called *theonomy*. This is the belief that morality is to be directed by God's law; *Theos* means God and *nomos* means law so it literally means "God's Law."[8] It is a rich term with great meaning presenting a specific Biblical theory of ethics where God's law governs.[9] This view of Biblical ethics is that "God's law as revealed in Scripture is the only proper rule and the only proper standard for human action."[10] It takes seriously all the law-commands found in Scripture in both Testaments.

---

8   Ibid., 16.

9   This writer embraces theonomy as an ethical theory but recognizes the complexity and the challenges that it creates in its application to civil society. Reconstructionism includes presuppositional apologetics, post-millenialism, and the use of Biblical civil law directives as necessary components along with theonomy to reconstruct the culture. Theonomy is an ethical theory held by all Reconstructionists. However, one can be a theonomist without being a Reconstructionist. Reconstructionism creates great debate and controversy over the details and application of Biblical case law and how to apply it.

10 Einwecter, 19-20.

"Theonomy teaches that the standard of Christian ethics is the whole Word of God from Genesis to Revelation. The law of God is revealed by Moses and the Prophets, and by Jesus and the Apostles."[11]

During the last quarter of the twentieth century theonomy became a relatively controversial term in American Christian circles because it became exclusively associated with a small group of men who specifically linked the ethical theory of theonomy to a social theory known as Reconstructionism which promotes the necessity of rebuilding society along the lines of the Old Testament law. Reconstruction and theonomy are closely linked but are not the same thing because theonomy is a significant *moral* theory and is not identical with Reconstructionism which is a *social* theory. This association and controversy should not allow Christians to think less of the great value found in God's law or less of the concept of theonomy. As Rousas Rushdoony[12] often observed, there is no real alternative in ethics but that of theonomy or autonomy, God's law or the law made by humans free from divine constraints. The theonomist understands that the human approach to right and wrong must relate

11 Ibid., 39.
12 Rousas Rushdoony is the greatest and most prominent voice of Reconstructionism, and a leader among the theonomists.

fundamentally to what God demands of us. These demands must be based on God's own character or what God Himself is, otherwise they are arbitrary, relative, and constructed by humans.

It is common to run into Christians who reject the relevance of God's law for morality by arguing that the law has been replaced by the Gospel. They want to pit the Old Testament law of God against the New Testament Gospel, thus making the Old Testament moral law only relevant to convict one of sin. But this is absurd; law and Gospel are not opponents. The moral law is never to be destroyed. It is eternal since it is demonstrative of God's nature and character. For the moral law of God to change, God's character would need to necessarily change. There is no teaching in the Bible that the moral law is to be obliterated. Jesus even stated that He had not come to destroy the law, but rather to satisfy its demands. He says in Matthew 5:17-18,

> "Do not think that I came to abolish the law or the Prophets; I did not come to abolish but to fulfill. For truly I say to you, until heaven and earth pass away, not the smallest letter or stroke shall pass from the law until all is accomplished."

He was not an opponent of the law. He did not come to "loosen it" in any way. Rather He loved

it, obeyed the law and fulfilled its demands completely.

It is thus my presumption that our obligation
is

> "to obey any Old Testament commandment
> unless the New Testament indicates otherwise.
> We must assume continuity with the Old Tes-
> tament rather than discontinuity. This is not to
> say that there are no changes from Old to New
> Testament."[13]

There are significant changes and differences.
Obviously there are advances and changes that
God makes under the New Covenant.

> "However, the word of God must be the stan-
> dard which defines precisely what those
> changes are for us; we cannot take it upon our-
> selves to assume such changes or read them into
> the New Testament."[14]

Some laws and practices are clearly set aside, but
not the eternal moral law that is demonstrative of
His character and grounded in His attributes.
Biblical revelation is progressive, but we must

> "be committed to the rule that the New Testa-
> ment should interpret the Old Testament for
> us; the attitude of Jesus and the Apostles to the

---

13 Bahnsen, *By This Standard*, 3.
14 Ibid.

Mosaic law, for instance, must be determinative of the Christian ethic."[15]

"Law commands and demands, it propounds what the will of God is. The law of God is the holiness of God coming to expression for the regulation of thought and conduct consonant with his holiness. We must be perfect as God is perfect; the law is that which the perfection of God dictates in order to bring about conformity with his perfection. Law pronounces approval and blessing upon conformity to its demands .... Law pronounces the judgment of condemnation upon every infraction of its precept."[16]

But there are a variety of Biblical laws. What about Old Testament holy days, feasts, and dietary laws? What about blood sacrifices of animals? What about the civil punishments for rebellious children? Do they all have equal authority for humans to obey today?

Three Types of Old Testament Law

Old Testament Biblical law is generally divided into three categories: the moral, the civil, and the ceremonial law. A large body of legislation was given to Moses on Mount Sinai and included what we now call civil, criminal, and domestic law, as well as ethical injunctions and

15 Ibid., 4.
16 Murray, 184.

extensive civil directions.[17] Certain aspects of these are no longer authoritative.

> "God gave certain localized imperatives to the (Jews)—commands for specified use in one concrete situation …. An example would be the command to go to war and gain the land of Palestine by the sword; this is not an enduring requirement for us today."[18]

CEREMONIAL LAW

Ceremonial law primarily refers to the sacrificial system of the old covenant or Old Testament which includes the cleanliness codes and the dietary restrictions.[19] Concerning the ceremonial law the *Westminster Confession* reads,

> "Besides this law, commonly called moral, God was pleased to give to the people of Israel, as a church under age, ceremonial laws, containing several typical ordinances, partly of worship, prefiguring Christ, His graces, actions, sufferings, and benefits; and partly, holding forth divers instructions of moral duties. All which

---

17 Bernard J. Bamberger, "Torah as God's Revelation to Israel" in *Great Jewish Ideas*, edited by Abraham Millgram, B'Nai B'Rith Adult Jewish Education Publishers, Washington D.C., 1964, p. 63.

18 Bahnsen, *By This Standard*, 5.

19 Richard D. Phillips, "Which Old Testament Laws Must I Obey?" http//www.tenth.org/qbox/qb_000806.htm, 1.

ceremonial laws are now abrogated, under the New Testament."[20]

Rightly practicing the ceremonial laws was considered a means of reestablishing a right relationship to God. By adhering to these specific regulations which include such things as observing Holy Days like the Sabbath, practicing circumcision, and celebrating ritualistic meals like Passover one could be purified. Sacrificial laws are still valid, they have not passed into oblivion, but because Christ died once for all, the sacrificial laws have been fulfilled. Other laws not considered binding have to do with cleanness and uncleanness, dietary laws, feast days, and religious ceremonies. These are still valid and have meaning, but both the laws and their sanctions have been fulfilled through Christ's death on the cross.[21]

In the New Testament examples of certain dietary and sacrificial practices are set aside. The Biblical book of Hebrews describes in detail how these ceremonial laws were merely a "shadow" of what was to come and they were fulfilled in

20 *Westminster Confession of Faith*, Chapter XIX, III, which affirms Old Testament Israel, the people of God, as the Church before Christ and that since Christ satisfies or fulfills all the Old Testament ceremonial laws, these laws no longer need to be practiced.

21 Jay Rogers, "What is Theonomy?" in *The Forerunner*, http://www.forerunner.com/theonomy/theofaq.html, 6.

Christ and are thus no longer necessarily practiced. Humans no longer need to make personal animal sacrifice as the payment for their sins because Christ completed this once and for all so there no longer remains a need for a sacrifice for sins. In reference to the fulfillment of the ceremonial law, Hebrews 10:1 reads,

> "For the law, since it has only a shadow of the good things to come and not the very form of things, can never by the same sacrifices year by year, which they offer continually, make perfect those who draw near."

Still in Hebrews 10 in verses 11-12 in reference to Jesus it says,

> "And every priest stands daily ministering and offering time after time the same sacrifices, which can never take away sins; but He, having offered one sacrifice for sins for all time, sat down at the right hand of God."

Ceremonial law is no longer in need of fulfillment. It has been completed in Christ.

CIVIL LAW

The civil law is a second category of law. These are the Biblical laws represented in the criminal code. *Westminster* says of them, God gave

"to them also, as a body politic, He gave sundry
judicial laws, which expired together with the
State of that people; not obliging under any
now, further than the general equity thereof
may require."[22]

These are actually applications of the moral law
to the sphere of civil jurisdiction to the nation of
Israel and many of them involve forms of restitu-
tion. These include consequences for criminal
behavior, such as for murder, theft, or negli-
gence. There is great debate among theologians
as to their relevance to nations other than Israel
and for their use in national governance. God is
to be God of the nations, and as such the moral
laws expressed through the practices found in
Old Testament civil law should provide guidance
in civil law-making. Certainly because of the
longstanding value of the moral law these should
be given great weight in understanding the civil
application of the moral law and as such provide
specific direction for civil authority and guidance
to any nation seeking justice in its national
sphere. Phillips questions, "Having God's
revealed law, why should any man wish to form a
moral and civil law out of the fallen and per-
verted elements of man's mind?"[23] The principles
that can be demonstrated and derived from Bibli-

---

22 Phillips, p.2.
23 Ibid., 684.

cal civil law certainly have relevance for all nations. If God's law is denied then the only universal law is imperialistic.[24]

We often find case law interspersed in with the ceremonial and moral law in these sections of Scripture. For example the Bible makes a good distinction between accidental manslaughter and malicious murder. This is illustrated by the example of a flying axe head in Deuteronomy 19:4-6, which reads,

> "Now this is the case of the manslayer who may flee there and live: when he kills his friend unintentionally, not hating him previously—as when a man goes into the forest with his friend to cut wood, and his hand swings the axe to cut down the tree, and the iron head slips off the handle and strikes his friend so that he dies—he may flee to one of these cities and live."

This situation may infrequently occur today, but there is a principle of manslaughter demonstrated here that has ongoing relevance.

> "What is of permanent authority is the principle illustrated, and not the cultural detail used to illustrate it. Thus we ought not to read the case laws of the Old Testament as binding us to the literal wording utilized (for example, …

---

24 Rushdoony, 17.

faulty car brakes would also be covered by the
law dealing with the flying axe head).[25]

It makes good sense that there should be contemporary relevance and application of the Old Testament civil law since it is reflective of the moral
law. Civil law must have some standard. And that
standard is either human autonomy or it is Biblical law.[26] When the moral law of God is codified
into civil law, it works to apply justice and to
restrain the passions of rebellious citizens.

Old Testament Moral Law

The third and most relevant form of Old
Testament law for ethics is God's moral law.
Many people including most Christians have no
understanding of the value or the importance of
Biblical moral law. The moral law found in
Scripture is an exact representation of the moral
nature and character of God. It speaks of who
God is; it is demonstrative and expressive of
God's nature. It is absolute, unchanging, and is
the righteousness of God revealed.

Psalm 19:7-9 says of God's moral law:

"The law of the Lord is perfect, restoring the
soul; The testimony of the Lord is sure, making
wise the simple. The precepts of the Lord are
right, rejoicing the heart; The commandment

---

25 Bahnsen, *By This Standard*, 5.
26 Rogers, 5.

of the Lord is pure, enlightening the eyes. The fear of the Lord is clean, enduring forever; The judgments of the Lord are true, they are righteous altogether."

These moral laws are to be learned, studied, comprehended, and memorized. Joshua 1:8 states,

"This book of the law shall not depart from your mouth, but you shall meditate upon it day and night, so that you may be careful to do all that is written in it; for then you will make your way prosperous and then you will have success."

And the *Westminster Confession* says,

"God gave to Adam a law, as a covenant of works, by which He bound him and all his posterity, to personal, entire, exact, and perpetual obedience, promised life upon the fulfilling, and threatened death upon the breach of it, and endued him with power and ability to keep it. This law, after his fall, continues to be a perfect rule of righteousness; and, as such, was delivered by God upon Mount Sinai, in ten commandments, and written in two tables: the first four commandments containing our duty towards God; and the other six, our duty to man."[27]

The law of Moses is part of a treaty or covenant (deep personal agreement or contract)

---

27 *Westminster Confession of Faith*, Chapter XIX: I,II..

between God and humans requiring an exclusive commitment to God. It must be obeyed in its totality and any violation of the law is an offense against God. The Ten Commandments are the primary stipulations given by God, and are broad premises or principles that carry with them blessing on those who obey, and cursing (a sense of judgment) on those who do not obey. Heaven and earth are witnesses and the summary of these on the tablets of stone, which are given to Israel through Moses, serve as a reminder of the agreement with God.

The direct, clear, moral commands given by God in the Scriptures used to be common knowledge in Western society. The Ten Commandments were once regularly recited and memorized in public classrooms but that is not the case anymore. Knowledge of God's commandments was respected, and in combination with a healthy fear of the Lord often functioned to restrain evil in society. But they are no longer remembered or understood as valuable. Most people today have little knowledge of them. Over the years I have often asked my classes to recite the Ten Commandments, and it is shocking how few students can list them. Below are the universally applicable Ten Commandments given to Moses as stated in Exodus 20:3-17:

"You shall have no other gods before Me. You shall not make for yourself an idol, or any likeness of what is in heaven above or on the earth beneath or in the water under the earth. You shall not worship them or serve them; for I, the Lord you God, am a jealous God, visiting the iniquity of the fathers on the children, on the third and the fourth generations of those who hate Me, but showing lovingkindness to thousands, to those who love Me and keep My commandments. You shall not take the name of the Lord your God in vain, for the Lord will not leave him unpunished who takes His name in vain. Remember the Sabbath and keep it holy. Six days you shall labor and do all your work, but the seventh day is a Sabbath of the Lord your God; in it you shall not do any work, you or your son or your daughter, your male servant or your female servant or your cattle or your sojourner who stays with you. For in six days the Lord made the heavens and the earth, and the sea and all that is in them, and rested on the seventh day; therefore the Lord blessed the Sabbath day and made it holy. Honor your father and your mother, that your days may be prolonged in the land which the Lord your God gives you. You shall not murder. You shall not commit adultery. You shall not steal. You shall not bear false witness against your neighbor. You shall not covet your neighbor's house; you shall not covet your neighbor's wife or his male servant or his fe-

male servant or his ox or his donkey or anything that belongs to your neighbor."

The divisions between the three types of law
(ceremonial, civil, and moral) presented here are use-
ful but there are limitations to this three-fold division
of law. It is a useful but overly simplistic division,
and the types of law often overflow into one
another so that some laws are in more than one
category, such as Sabbath laws which are found
in each of the three law categories. For example,
there are aspects of the Sabbath that apply to all
three types of law: ceremonial, civil, and moral,
which makes it a complex issue that cannot be
adequately addressed here. Because of this there is
still widespread disagreement on the applicability
of the Sabbath. Some say since it is among the
Ten Commandments, then it is moral law and
binding. Others quote Colossians 2:16-17,

"Therefore let no one act as your judge in regard to food or drink or in respect to a festival
or a new moon or a Sabbath day—things which
are a shadow of what is to come,"

to support the fulfillment of the Sabbath by Jesus.
There is certainly a proper Biblical principle to
honor God with a day of the week. In the New
Testament this is referred to as "The Lord's Day,"
and the Church gathers on this first day of the
week. It makes sense to set the first day apart for

worship since life should begin with God. In the book of Hebrews Jesus is called "our Sabbath Rest." As such He fulfills the ceremonial aspect of the Sabbath laws and we can find our rest in Him. Concerning the observance of dietary restrictions and special days, Romans 14:5 adds, "Let each man be convinced in his own mind." Applying this principle to the Sabbath one could certainly argue that there are principles of the Sabbath that can be carried over and practiced by Christians according to their consciences.[28]

"God's moral law is revealed in the context of case laws, historical narrative, prophecy, psalms, proverbs, gospels, and epistles .... (It) is made known in all parts of the Word of God."[29] The three types of law found in the Old Testament are still binding today except where they have been fulfilled or overturned by the commands of the New Testament. Passages such as Proverbs 3:5-7 and Psalm 19 also emphasize the perfect unchanging nature and value of God's moral law. It is all appropriate for godly instruction. So the Ten Commandments do not stand alone as the revealed law of God, but they stand as the core of Biblical morality and are part of an explicit for-

---

28 I believe that solid biblical arguments can be made for the church meeting on the first day of the week for worship based on the argument that Christ was raised on the first day and that the early church met on the first day.

29 Einwechter, 39.

mal law code that all should follow. Those who
fail to keep them in their entirety become
covenant-breakers who are placed under God's
judgment.

New Testament Law

All of Scripture is the basis for law, not
merely the Old Testament. There are many law
commands given in the New Testament. The
New Testament has rescinded certain aspects of
the Mosaic law, such as religious ceremonies,
feasts, and dietary laws, but there are obvious
moral commands given in the New Testament.
In Matthew 5:44 we are commanded to love our
enemies and to do good to those who hate us. In
1 John 2:15 it says to love not the world or the
things of the world. Colossians 3:15 says to
always be thankful. Romans 12 has a long list of
statements that are really law-commands: "Let
love be without hypocrisy. Abhor what is evil;
cling to what is good. Be devoted to one another
in brotherly love; give preference to one another
in honor" and many more. Over a thousand New
Testament commands can be found. The New
Testament law commands are most explicitly
stated in what is sometimes referred to as the
"laws of love." Matthew records this interaction
with Jesus when a lawyer asks Him,

> "'Teacher, which is the great commandment in
> the law?' And He said to him, 'You shall love
> the Lord your God with all your heart, and
> with all your soul, and with all your mind. This
> is the great and foremost commandment. And a
> second is like it, You shall love your neighbor
> as yourself'" (Matthew 5:17-19).

Though these are less specific than the commands
given in the Mosaic law, they are nevertheless
law commands that are to be obeyed. Jesus
always emphasized the validity of the law and
certainly focused on His own mission to fulfill
the law.

The law of God is perfect and holy, but there
are some things that the law is incapable of
doing. The law cannot legally justify the law-
breaker. No one is saved by obedience to the law,
whether it is moral, civil, or ceremonial law.
Many in the Christian tradition have shied away
from love for God's law because they associate
this with **legalism**, the belief that following the
law is paramount for obtaining salvation. But the
law cannot redeem anyone. Theonomists do not
believe anyone is saved by the moral law; the law
is valuable for instruction in ethics. Paul
adamantly counters the legalism of the Judaizers
in the book of Galatians when the Judaizers
emphasize the need for Christians to become
Jews first through circumcision. Martin Luther
rightly reacts against legalism during the Refor-

mation, responding contrary to the acts of penance through the selling of indulgences established by the Roman Catholic Church to achieve forgiveness. In response to both forms of legalism practiced by Judaizers and indulgence-sellers Paul and Luther emphasize salvation is never achieved by obedience to the law or by works. The law is unforgiving and hard as nails, and all attempts to follow it flawlessly fail. It does not have the capability to set a person free from the bondage to sin. It is unable to change the human heart; another way must be found to become free. Romans 7:1-4 describes how one must become free from the law as a means of salvation if one is to become joined to Christ. So when the Scriptures teach the need to be free from the law, it means to be free from the penalty of the law, to be free from the law's condemnation or the curse of the law. The law never sets anyone free from evil. But neither does Scripture intend for us to ignore the law or release us from its moral obligations. Contrary to much popular thought, "the alternative to law is not grace; it is lawlessness."[30]

Modern Christians resist the notion of a God who is holy, just, righteous, and full of indignation toward those who ignore His law commands. Some do not like God's law because it creates a fear of God that is not consistent with

---

30 Rushdoony, 20.

our shallow, contemporary, grandfatherly, Santa Claus image of God. Rather than asking whether we should obey God, it is often mistakenly asked how can God make me happy.[31] When was the last time you heard someone publicly proclaim that it "is a terrifying thing to fall into the hands of the living God" (Hebrews 10:31)?

THE FALL OF HUMANITY

God declared to the first humans the first law command, "You shall not eat of the tree of the knowledge of good and evil." Adam and Eve were warned that if they disobeyed they would die. But they did not heed God's lawful warning and ate anyway. Due to Adam's disobedience to God's first explicit directive, Adam hid himself from God because Adam had immediately died spiritually; he had become fallen, damaged and dead to God. "The wages of sin is death," declares Romans 6:23, and this became true for Adam. He experiences true moral guilt for sin and spiritual death through his rebellion. This estrangement experienced by Adam and Eve is transmitted to all their progeny so that humans are unable to honor God properly due to their spiritual death. Their individual act of disobedience becomes

---

31 No author listed. "Justification by Faith and Christian Ethics" in *Present Truth Magazine*, vol. 13 – Article 4, http://www.presenttruthmag.com/archive/XIII/13-4.htm, 3.

ours. "In the fall (of Adam and Eve) two things are to be considered: the committing of the transgression and its propagation."[32] This is an inborn, ongoing condition in all humans subsequent to Adam, and is called original sin.[33]

To be alienated from God is to be under God's wrath or judgment, and impotent to correct this condition through any human efforts. Various Christian traditions interpret differently how damaged human nature is, but all understand humanity to be abnormal and damaged by sin, resulting in a sinful condition. This doctrine of original sin is described in Jeremiah 17:9, "The heart is more deceitful than all else and is desperately sick." Genesis 8:21 says, "The intent of man's heart is evil from his youth." The heart is antagonistic toward God; Colossians 1:21 expresses this alienation by calling us the "enemies" of God. There exists a moral flaw in humanity that extends to every part of his being. By God's standards every human is corrupt and wicked. This is the defacement of the image of God. Those who think of humans as intrinsically good have a very low view of good and are terribly deceived. The image of God remains, but it is dreadfully damaged or distorted. As a result

32 William Ames, *The Marrow of Theology*, (Durham, NC: The Labyrinth Press, 1968), 114.

33 Other terms for original sin are "fallen," "in Adam," "in sin," "in the flesh," and "spiritually dead."

humans use reason not to glorify God, but to rise up in arrogant opposition to the knowledge of God.[34] We become autonomous and a law to ourselves.[35] Evil deeds, thoughts, and attitudes spring from a corrupt heart.

Sin is an attitude, character, condition, or act in violation of God's law arising from the heart of a rational creature. Jesus declared that it is not what goes into a man that defiles him, but what comes out, i.e. evil thoughts, fornication, theft, murder, coveting, etc. (Mark 7:18). The book of Proverbs announces, "As a man ponders in his heart, so is he." It is obvious in Scripture and in human practice that the sinfulness of humanity comes from within and does not begin from without. This is why there is the spiritual and moral necessity for a change of heart, so that one's actions proceed from a heart of faith and not unbelief, a heart that is alive to God and not dead.

> "Created 'in the image of God,' innocent and righteous at first, our parents fell from original righteousness and became sinful and corrupt. And from that day to this all men and women are born in the image of fallen Adam and Eve, and inherit a heart and nature inclined to evil."[36]

---

34 Bahnsen, *Always Ready*, 46.
35 Ibid.
36 John Charles Ryle, *Holiness*, Part One (Pensacola:

The nature of the fruit indicates the nature of the tree.

Adam is the prototype and like Adam, humans continue to willingly choose to disobey God's law commands. This is our actual sin or personal acts of disobedience to God's law.

> "'A sin' … consists in doing, saying, thinking, or imagining, anything that is not in perfect conformity with the mind and law of God. 'Sin,' in short, as the Scripture saith, is 'the transgression of the law' (1 John 3:4). The slightest, outward or inward departure from absolute mathematical parallelism with God's revealed will and character constitute a sin, and at once makes us guilty in God's sight."[37]

These violations place humans under God's judgment, in debt to God for their personal disobedience and immorality. No one is exempt, as Romans 3:23 says, "All have sinned and fall short of the glory of God," and Romans 3:10, "There is none who is righteous, no not one." Humans try to fool themselves into thinking that we are not so very bad, but this is very deceptive. Humans put off an odor of sin, but are like animals whose smell is most offensive to humans but the animals themselves have no idea that they are offensive, and are not offensive to each another.

Chapel Library, 2001), 15.
37 Ibid., 14.

We should understand that there are not just sins of commission or acts in disobedience to God's law, but also sins of omission when we fail to love as we ought.

> "I need not tell a careful student of the New Testament, that there are sins of omission as well as commission, and that we sin, as our Prayer-book reminds us, by 'leaving undone the things we ought to do,' as really as by 'doing the things we ought not to do.' … It is there written (in the Gospel of Matthew) 'Depart ye cursed, into everlasting fire: for I was hungry and ye gave me no meal; I was thirsty, and ye gave me no drink'" (Matthew 25:41-42).[38]

So all humans stand universally condemned because each person directly rebels against God and His law by breaking God's commandments and sinning against a Holy God in acts of commission and omission, and each person is born into sin, fallen and spiritually separated from God.

Optimistic humanism offers no hope for modern humans and should have died a generation ago. G. K. Chesterton once remarked that the only Christian doctrine that is empirically verifiable is the doctrine of original sin. Is it not obvious to any student of history? It has been the failure of humans to acknowledge the reality of

---

38 Ibid.

human evil and sin that has put all human ethical developments in conflict with the Christian ethic. Our rebellion against God and His law not only shatters the relationship with God and brings God's justice into view, but shatters the relationships between humans.

It is impossible to separate moral guilt and condemnation from sin. This moral condition manifests itself by the consequence of death. Death is "ordained as a vengeance upon sin."[39] It is abhorred by the living, yet it must be understood as a judgment upon human rebellion against God. C. S. Lewis describes how death should exclaim to the living that something is wrong with the world.[40] Death is a form of judgment, is always an abnormal separation, and is understood in three ways: (1) spiritual death, which is original sin or the fallen human condition of being separated relationally from God; (2) physical death, which is the abnormal separation of soul from body; (3) and eternal death, the everlasting separation of the self from God, also called Hell. Hell is this estrangement from God carried into eternity. These are the consequence of sin and God's judgment upon sinners for their law-breaking, unrighteous, immoral activity. The universal condition of humanity is that law-

---

39 Ames, 116.
40 Lewis, *The Problem of Pain*, Chapters 5-6.

breakers are in a fallen state and are incapable of obeying God. The will is deprived of being able to will the holy. Nevertheless, humans are still accountable and responsible to God for all personal actions of breaking God's law, i.e. their sins, and all suffer the same punishment of death.

THE THREE MAJOR ROLES BIBLICAL MORAL LAW PLAYS

Biblical law is as relevant today for ethics as it has ever been. The Psalmist writes, "Thy righteous judgments endure forever" (Ps. 119:60). Without God's moral law as a light, humans are left morally lost. Since the Reformation it has generally been agreed upon that the law of God has three primary purposes. The first is as a "school master" or "tutor" to convict a person of sin (Galatians 3:24) so that one might be led to Christ. The law informs humans of God's holy moral and righteous character and acts as a measuring stick to reveal to them their own flawed moral behavior, thus giving them a clear knowledge of sin. James 2:10 declares that, "For whoever keeps the whole law and yet stumbles in one point, he has become guilty of all." When the law is broken at a single point, the covenantal relationship with God is broken and the law becomes an instrument of condemnation. One comes under the "curse" of the law. Through the commands of the law one learns to know their own personal shortcomings and moral failures. The purpose of God's law is to expose human failure and prove we are sinners through and through.[41] In Romans 7 Paul recognizes he would never have become acutely aware of his own sinfulness if he had not read the law's command not to covet. This awareness of the law's commands should lead to reflection on how to satisfy the law since it must be fulfilled. When humans find themselves unable to achieve justification or to rightly obey the commands of the law it should stir them to understand their need for forgiveness and redemption, and drive them to Christ. The law awakens us to the desperateness of sin and the urgency of finding a Savior.

The moral law brings conviction of sin and condemnation. Christ holds up God's law as a mirror that we may see ourselves as God sees us. I look into a mirror and see that my face is dirty, but I don't use the mirror to wash my face. It would be foolishness to take the mirror down and rub my dirty face with it. The purpose of the mirror is not to clean the face, but to reveal the dirt. The purpose of the mirror is to send the person with a dirty face to the water to wash. The mirror does not clean. It only reveals. Similarly, anyone who tries to be saved by keeping the Ten Commandments or living by the Sermon on the

---

41 Phillip A. Ross, *Practically Christian: Applying James To-
    day*, (Marietta, OH, Pilgrim Platform, 2001, 2007), 55.

Mount is like a person who tries to wash with a mirror. It cannot be done. He will only smear the dirt on his face and smudge the mirror in the process. God's law is like a mirror, it reveals human sin. But it cannot cleanse the sin.[42] True moral guilt should lead one to Christ for forgiveness and salvation.

A second use of the law is cultural; it is a social restraint and sets standards on how every society should live if its people are to be moral. It teaches the art of living rightly. When the moral law is written down it strengthens and reinforces the unwritten law on the heart. It pricks the conscience. The principles it sets forth have this practical value for all times and all cultures. This law given to Moses sets the standard for personal, family, church, and societal ethics, and under the law the total moral life of humans is to be ordered. It restrains even wicked men from doing every wicked thing that they might. The law can teach men to fear God and thus hesitate before doing evil. It provides a basis for a just and well-ordered society, and it should guide all of our relationships to others since it morally binds all humans in all ages.[43] As we observe the moral decline in society we might ask what has caused this. Certainly there are multiple causes, but one

---

42 Ibid., 38.
43 Einwecter, 90.

contributing factor is the current neglect for and ignorance of God's moral law. Society has forgotten the pedagogical value of God's law, and as such has seen the consequence in the moral degeneration of society.

The third role of the law is to provide a rule of life and a moral standard for Christians. It is a means of grace for sanctification of the Christian, for it is the rule of life for the believer, showing him or her how to conduct their lives. It pictures what a sanctified Christian life looks like and is a guide to believers in their daily walk. A Christian life where one is "walking by the Spirit" will never be a life in contradiction to God's law. Many have neglected these latter two uses, but they should not be negated, and neither is there any Biblical support to do so.

No Lawful Hope for Humanity

The law is God's righteousness. It is holy and beautiful. It is perfect in every way. It serves as a standard to expose human sin, it sets the standards for family and civil living, and it shows the Christian what a sanctified life should look like. But there are things the law cannot do. Biblical law can never create righteousness or provide any human the power to resist sin. Neither can it create obedience or empower one to live accordingly. It has no ability to justify the law-breaker. It is incapable of creating sanctification, though it communicates what a sanctified life should look like. But there is nothing inherently wrong with God's law. The problem lies within the wicked human heart.

4. CURE FOR THE MORAL FLAW

RESTORATION

Humans are spiritually dead, estranged from God and in continuous rebellion against God's law. God demands complete righteousness and obedience, yet humans fail and come under judgment. Human works and deeds can never reestablish this relationship. If one understands the infinite holiness of God, the nature of His perfect law, and the utter depravity of humans, then a person can begin to understand how desperate the human condition is. Evil is a reality and it flourishes in the rebellious human heart and manifests itself in immoral behavior. Furthermore there is nothing we can do ourselves to fix it. Humans are in this desperate state of condemnation as law-breakers, but "sin is more than breaking God's law. It is aggravated assault upon the infinite dignity of (God's) person." Humans are lawless covenant-breakers under God's condemnation and deserving of His wrath.[1] This constitutes true moral guilt.

While humans are in this hopeless and help-less condition alienated from God, Jesus, who is fully God, became fully human. He lives a sinless life of complete obedience to God's law, thereby achieving all righteousness and being undeserv-ing of death. Jesus became God's ultimate act of special revelation (Hebrews 1:1). Jesus is tempted like us in all respects only without sin, says Hebrews 4:15. His life is morally exemplary, but more than this, He completely upholds the law's authority (Matthew 5:17). He is the lamb without moral blemish. He perfectly demonstrates the quality of moral love and fulfills all righteousness through His perfect obedience to God's moral law.[2] He claims not to nullify the law but to fulfill it. Jesus is without sin, submissive to the Father and the law in active obedience. Nevertheless, Jesus suffers the judgment of God that sinners deserve even though He was not a sinner (i.e. not a moral law-breaker). The "wages of sin is death" but since Jesus did not sin, He did not deserve death. His death is a voluntary sacrifice or cover-

---

1 Jerry Bridges, "What is Grace?"
   http://rq.rts.edu/fall98/grace.html, 3.
2 Christ's active obedience is considered living his whole life in perfect accord with Biblical law. His passive obe-dience is His willingness to obey the Father in submit-ting to His death on the cross.

ing for sin. He suffers the judgment of God that
sinners deserve. Carl Henry calls the cross "the
center of the moral universe, unveiling God's
absolute refusal to suspend His law of holiness."[3]

Jesus gives up His life as a propitiation[4] or
sacrifice for sin dying a shameful death in our
place on the cross. Romans 5:8 says, "While we
were yet sinners Christ died for us." **This is
GRACE, God's undeserved gift to humans.**
"Grace means that the conditions of salvation are
in God's hands alone."[5] Now, all who place faith
in Him can stand forgiven and have their sinfulness transferred to Christ. God could not just turn
His back on human sin and pretend it did not
exist. This would compromise His justice and
holiness. Far too many think of God as nonjudg-
mental and one who will forgive our sins uncon-
ditionally without regard for justice. This
opposes God's just, yet loving nature. God "cannot exercise mercy at the expense of His justice.
He cannot choose simply to overlook sin because
He feels sorry for us. God's justice must be satis-
fied."[6]

Jesus pays the penalty of death on the cross
for the sins of those who place faith in Him. This

---

3   Carl Henry, *Personal Christian Ethics*, 367.
4   *Propitiation* is a payment or sacrifice made.
5   Ross, 53.
6   Bridges, 4.

is called substitutionary atonement and is God's means of restoration and redemption.

> "The death of Christ is the last act of his humiliation in which he undergoes extreme, horrible, and most acute pain for the sins of men ... it equals all the misery the sins of men deserved."[7]

Those who accept this act of grace[8] by placing faith (belief and trust) in Jesus receive the forgiveness of sins. Ephesians 2:8-9 reads,

> "For by grace you have been saved through faith; and that not of yourselves, it is the gift of God not as a result of works, so that no one may boast."

The person of faith also receives a regenerated, new heart inclined toward God, replacing the condition of spiritual death or original sin. Of this new birth Paul writes, "If anyone is in Christ He is a new creation," (1 Corinthians 5:21). Additionally, their sins are now covered or forgiven.

> "The Biblical doctrine of atonement undergirds all Christian ethics. It shows us that God was not only providing for the justification of sinners, but for the justification of the moral order

---

7   Ames, 141.

8   *Grace* is unmerited favor. It is receiving a gift that is undeserved. Theologically grace is when God does any act of goodness toward those who are underserving.

of the universe. It shows us that the divine law
and government must be maintained and vin-
dicated."[9]

The death of Jesus is the proper compensation.
He satisfies the conditions of righteousness and
fulfills the need for justice. He turns away the
wrath of God from us by bearing the consequences of sin on Himself. Mercy is thus
extended to believers without subverting God's
justice.[10]

Salvation is by the act of God alone and is by
grace through faith. Grace is receiving a gift. It is
not receiving what one deserves but receiving
God's favor, though one does not deserve it. It is
coming to know one's forgiveness and to no
longer have a consciousness of sin and to "see our
sins as God sees them: judged, paid for, buried,
and gone."[11] Romans 8:1 declares, "There is
therefore now no condemnation for those who
are in Christ Jesus." God announces to the justified one, "Acquitted."

Christian salvation is made effectual by faith
alone in Christ. By this means alone one becomes
lawfully justified. Justification is a legal term

---

9   Justification by Faith and Christian Ethics," no author listed,
    The Forerunner, http://www.forerunner.com/theonomy/theo-
    faq.html, 6
10 Bridges, 4.
11 Pete Guilquist, *Love is Now*, (Grand Rapids: Zondervan, 1970),
    29.

meaning acquitted of all charges and Christianity teaches that a person is justified by **faith alone**.

> "Wherefore it ought to be the very first concern of every Christian to lay aside all trust in works, and more and more to strengthen faith alone, and through faith to grow in the knowledge, not of works, but of Christ Jesus."[12]

One is not saved by works, laws, or ceremonies. It is faith in Christ that fulfills the law and makes one righteous before God.

Humans cannot gain God's approval through any actions, for that is legalism; it is only by faith that God is pleased. Those who accept this act of grace by placing faith in Jesus receive the forgiveness of sins and a regenerated new nature favorable toward God. Both human ethical problems are dealt with as one is forgiven and receives a new nature. Paul phrased this exchange in a remarkable way. "He made Him who knew no sin to be sin on our behalf, so that we might become the righteousness of God in Him" (2 Corinthians 5:21). The restoration of humans is lifting them from a state of sin and death to a state of grace and life.[13]

---

12 Martin Luther, A Treatise on Christian Liberty, http://www.godrules.net/library/ludther/NEW1luther_b 6.htm, 9.

13 Ames, 128.

The instigator of the Reformation, Martin Luther, says in a direct address to the Pope,

> "This faith cannot at all exist in connection with works …. Therefore the moment you begin to believe, you learn that all things in you are altogether blameworthy, sinful and damnable, as Romans 3:23 says, 'For all have sinned and fall short of the glory of God;' and again, 'there is none just, there is none that doeth good, all have turned out of the way: they are become unprofitable together.' Who suffered and rose again for you, that, believing in Him, you may through this faith become a new man, in that all your sins are forgiven, and you are justified by the merits of another, namely, of Christ alone."[14]

Furthermore in the same tract Luther adds,

> "For not by the doing of works, but by believing do we glorify God and acknowledge that He is truthful. Therefore, faith alone is the righteousness of a Christian man and the fulfilling of all the commandments. For he who fulfills the First (Commandment), has no difficulty in fulfilling all the rest. But works, being insensate things, cannot glorify God, although they can, if faith be present, be done to the glory of God."[15]

---

14 Luther, 9.
15 Luther, 11.

5. MOTIVE MATTERS IN CHRISTIAN ETHICS

> *"As you therefore have received Christ Jesus the Lord, so walk in Him, having been firmly rooted and now being built up in Him and established in your faith, just as you were instructed, and overflowing with gratitude" (Colossians 2:6-7).*

Walking is a metaphor describing how the Christian life is to be lived. The Christian is to walk with Christ and to walk by faith in Him. This walking is slow and gradual, leading to a righteous way of living. In this passage a directive is given to Christians telling them to live like Christ, not for the purpose of becoming saved, but because one has been saved. God declares believers in Christ to be righteous, and now He instructs them to live this way. But what is the driving force or motive for living this new way?

A proper Biblical understanding of grace and forgiveness is directly related to Christian ethics.

For a Christian, the necessary motive for moral action is love. And the only way one is truly capable of doing a loving act is by first understanding the value of forgiveness, of directly and experientially knowing the love of God. This is understood through a proper intellectual understanding of the doctrine of grace and learning to live inspired by grace.

It is through God's acts of redemption that humans learn the way of love. Christian ethics is now living out of that new life and living for God, not in order to receive forgiveness, but out of love for God and a desire to please Him, motivated by His love and mercy. The twentieth century Dutch theologian, G. C. Berkouwer, states, "The essence of Christian theology is grace, and the essence of Christian ethics is gratitude."[1] We deserve wrath but instead we receive mercy in Christ. This is grace; this is love. Once we have the correct understanding of grace, then the necessary motivation for obedience to God is out of a thankful heart. Theology has a practical application for ethics. The great Puritan theologian, William Ames, begins his work, *The Marrow of Theology,* with the profound statement, "Theology is the doctrine or teaching of living to God."[2] A proper understanding of God and of

1   Bridges, 5.
2   Ames, 77.

Christian salvation through Christ's mercy is the reason one is driven to become moral. "It is gratitude arising spontaneously from a heart filled with grace that motivates us to obey God and serve Him wholeheartedly."[3]

Like Immanuel Kant, Christian ethics is interested in motives, but the motive in Christian ethics is not one of duty as Kant argues.[4] The Christian motive is love; an understanding and living out of a life of love is fundamental to Christian ethics. The person who understands the doctrine of grace and the breadth of God's mercy extended through the sacrificial atoning death of Jesus in our place can only respond in awe and exclaim, "How can I *not* love Him." Loving God is responsive; we love because He first loved us. This leads to a heart that now wants to obey Him. "If you love me, you will keep my commandments" (John 14:15), states Jesus. Love is the Christian motive for ethics but it is more than a sentimental feeling. It is deep emotion based on a rational decision that propels action. It ultimately

> "does not rest so much on our love for Christ as it does on Christ's love for us. It is His greater love that constrains us and urges us on to strive for righteousness in our ethical lives …. So

---

3 Bridges, 5.
4 Immanuel Kant, *Grounding of the Metaphysics of Morals*, (Indianapolis: Hackett Publishing Co., 1993), 7-9.

great a love elicits a response from its recipi-
ents."[5]

Because God declares us righteous in Christ, we
now are motivated to live practically in line with
that declaration.

It is possible for a person to demonstrate
interest in God's law and even desire to follow it
but still have a heart that is distant from God.
Human motives are often mixed and hard to
decipher. It is impossible to look into the hearts
of others and know the true reasons for their
actions. God, on the other hand, looks at the
human heart and understands it quite well. He
knows the motives for our actions. 1 Samuel 16:7
says,

> "But the Lord said to Samuel, 'Do not look at
> his appearance or at the height of his stature,
> because I have rejected him; for God sees not as
> man sees, for man looks at the outward appear-
> ance, but the Lord looks at the heart."

God knows the secret motives of the human
heart. The core Christian motive in ethics should
be love. No moral action is completely good
unless it is motivated by love. Learning to be
motivated by love does not take place overnight
but through a life of progressive spiritual growth.
Since loving God and loving one's neighbor are

5   Oswin Craton, "The Basis of Christian Ethics,"
     http://www.craton.net/ethics/part4.htm, 2.

the greatest Christian commandments, then it is very important to be motivated by love and to understand what love is.

First Corinthians 13:1-3 reinforces the importance of love and defines Biblical love,

> "If I speak with the tongues of men and of angels, but do not have love I have become a noisy gong or a clanging cymbal. And if I have the gift of prophecy, and know all mysteries and all knowledge, and if I have all faith, so as to remove mountains, but do not have love, I am nothing. And if I give all my possessions to feed the poor, and if I deliver my body to be burned, but do not have love, it profits me nothing."

Having spiritual gifts is good; having great faith is good; being generous and becoming a martyr is good, but they are nothing unless motivated by love. One should then conclude that obedience to the law and self-sacrificing actions have no value in themselves but only as they are driven by love. Apart from love they are empty actions.

In the New Testament tradition John is considered the Apostle of love. He writes in 1 John 4:7, 9:

> "Beloved, let us love one another, for love is from God; and everyone who loves is born of God and knows God …. By this the love of God was manifested in us, that God has sent

His only begotten Son into the world that we
might live through Him."

Christ is the example of love. John adds in verses
10 and 11, "In this is love, not that we loved God,
but that He loved us and sent His Son to be the
propitiation[6] for our sins. Beloved, if God so
loved us, we also ought to love one another."
From this foundational understanding comes the
response that, "we love because He first loved us."
Christian love is modeled by the unselfishness of
Jesus. He shows us what love is in action, that it is
concern for others over oneself. But it is more
than just a model. His Lordship over our lives
produces an internal change in the heart of the
person who is regenerated and has faith in Christ.
This person becomes progressively "other" cen-
tered rather than self-centered. Humans are not
inclined toward loving each other, but when one
accepts and understands the love of God in Christ
and the nature of unselfish love, then from this
foundation one is able to love others. "We love
because He first loved us" (1 John 4:19) becomes
more than a clever cliché; it becomes a lived-out
reality. This is the nature of Christian liberty:
God gives the freedom to love as we ought. The
response to God's love is to love Him with all

---

6   *Propitiation* means atonement, sacrifice, expiation or pay-
    ment for one's sins.

one's heart, soul, and might which generates into a love for one's neighbor.

> "Using modern counterparts to the Hebrew terms one might say love Him with your entire mind, all your emotions and every fraction of your physical power. For as God loves, so is He to be loved by the totality of each man. And that totality of man's responsive love is now spelled out."[7]

Converted humans who understand the love of Christ will work to increase goodness in the world and decrease the sorrow.

---

7   Lou H. Silberman, "God and Man," in *Great Jewish Ideas*, 157.

6. Living A Moral Christian Life

The Reality of living as a Christian

It sounds so easy; just follow God's law demands, motivated by the love for God. If moral living could only be as easy as it sounds by following these ten commands, but obviously it is not. All humans undergo struggles making moral decisions, but for Christians there is a different type of inner moral conflict that occurs. The intense reality of this in-depth internal warfare is expressed vividly in Romans 7. This chapter written by the remarkable, single-minded, apostle Paul sounds quite distressing. He describes his moral battle in v.15, "For what I am doing, I do not understand; for I am not practicing what I want to do, but I am doing the very thing I hate." Paul experiences the reality of the new birth by which the heart is spiritually regenerated. Paul is "in Christ" and has this new nature alive to God that desires to obey and follow God, but he also continues to be influenced by an old sinful nature that has not been totally rendered inactive. There is an evil principle still in him which he calls sin, causing him to do wrong even though he wants to do good.

Prior to conversion the old nature is in bondage to sin and it has dominion over Paul but now there is an alternative force for good at work. The Christian life is a life of conflict between these two natures. Due to this interior struggle between Paul's old fleshly fallen Adamic nature and his new godly nature, he cries out in despair, "Wretched man that I am! Who will set me free from the body of this death?" (Romans 7:14). He concludes this section stating, "I myself with my mind am serving the law of God, but on the other, with my flesh (the old nature) the law of sin" (Romans 7:25). The Christian undergoes a battle between these two natures and Paul's internal being is at war between his new inclinations and his old desires. However, there is now a real choice between following the old man or the new man since he is no longer in complete bondage to sin.

The moral Christian life is experiencing greater and greater victory by the new nature as one spiritually matures. This is called sanctification. **Sanctification is becoming set apart for God's purposes; it is becoming holy in practice.** Justification is a once-for-all definitive act, whereas sanctification is progressive. A sanctified life is one which gradually and consistently sees the new nature becoming dominant.

> "Sanctification is that inward spiritual work that the Lord Jesus Christ works in a man by the Holy Spirit when He calls him to be a true believer. He not only washes him from his sins ... He also separates him from his natural love of sin and the world, puts a new principle in his heart, and makes him practically godly in life."[1]

The law is not the dynamic power that brings about true obedience but it is only through the inner working of God's Spirit that this transition comes about. Though we may not be completely freed from the corruption of the fallen nature that remains in us, the life that is committed to Christ will find the old nature having less dominion over time. Sanctification will never prevent a human from having a great deal of internal spiritual conflict or struggle in the heart between the old and new natures, but there should be a progression toward the goal of rendering the old nature useless or powerless.

Living out a Christian life includes an inner clash between the old nature that is inherited from Adam and is the result of sin in conflict with the new nature given to one in Christ. Romans 7 describes the conflict between these

---

1   J.C. Ryle, *The Nature of Sanctification*, 8.

two natures until Paul ends this section with a great cry of relief in Romans 8:1, "There is therefore now no condemnation for those who are in Christ Jesus." This freedom from guilt and freedom from sin's dominion through justification leaves a person free to love and follow Christ.

> "Those who have hearts made right with God, those who have been given a new heart to please God, will seek to walk according to God's commandments (Jeremiah 31:33; Ezekiel 11:19-20; 36:26-27)."[2]

The old nature can never really be destroyed but it can be rendered ineffective or subdued. "The subjugation of indwelling sin so that it may not have power to bring forth the works of the flesh is the constant duty of the believer."[3] A Christian who continually gives way to the sinful nature will find joy missing from her life and will be ineffective in loving God and others. She will not lose her salvation but will be rendered joyless and ineffective. This affects the relationship with Christ, but should not affect salvation if faith is sincere. However, not living out faith in practice should certainly cause one to question the genuineness of faith. There is freedom from slavery

---

2 Bahnsen, *By This Standard*, 34.
3 A,W. Pink. "Mortification and Vivification," in *Sanctification*, Free Grae Broadcaster, Issue 215, Spring 2011, (Pensacola: Chapel Library, 2011), 24.

to sin. Spiritual and moral Christian growth will include counting oneself dead to sin, alive to God, and yielding to God. Once our obligation to follow sin ends we have to learn to become free from the sin nature. We are to reckon it or count it to be dead due to the merit of Christ. Perfection will never be achieved in this life, but moral improvement should be happening, not to achieve faith, not to become a Christian, not to find meritorious favor with God, but to demonstrate that one is a Christian, and out of gratitude and love for God.

Obedience to the Moral Law Remains a Part of Christian Ethics

The life that progresses by faith will find itself producing two types of effects. First there will be a greater desire to obey God and the moral law set forth in the Scriptures and secondly there will be an increase of the Fruit of the Spirit or what philosophers could call a life of virtue. A Christian is dead to the law as an indictment, as a legal sentence of death against him. For Christians the function of the law is no longer accusatory. Justification, a legal declaration by which a person is declared not guilty of law-breaking, is by grace through faith, and removes the penalty of law-breaking by placing the penalty of judgment and death on Christ. Justification sets one free to serve God and neighbor; but it does not destroy the

law. Though a person is justified apart from the
works of the law, the law remains the moral standard of right and wrong. The law has no salvific
value for those who are Christians, though it still
stands as a rule of conduct and is of great useful-
ness in showing believers in Christ how to live.
Remember that Jesus said that the fulfillment of
the law is found in loving God and loving one's
neighbor. Love fulfills Biblical law. Obedience to
God's law for the one with faith in God now
comes from the heart.

> "But when love is said to be the fulfillment of
> the law, it is the love to God that is in view ….
> And this must mean that the practice of the
> biblical ethos, the … bringing to expression
> and fruition of the behavior required and ap-
> proved by the biblical revelation, springs from
> this love."[4]

To the extent that love governs us it will produce
obedience to God's law commands.

> "Where there is the perfection of love there will
> be the perfection of both ethical character and
> behavior. Love never fails, and perfect love casts
> out fear."[5]

Love for God will never lead to actions contrary
to the law of God.

---

4   Murray, 21.
5   Ibid.

"The believer in Christ is released from the law as a ground of acceptance, but not as a standard of holiness."[6] The *Westminster Confession* says of the moral law, "The moral law doth forever bind all, as well justified persons as others, to the obedience thereof."[7] Any commitment to Christianity carries with it certain moral commands as a follow-up to this commitment. There is a current misunderstanding among many Christians that keeping the commandments of Scripture is too burdensome and not consistent with the freedom that Christ gives. They confuse keeping the law with legalism.

> "It is strange indeed that this kind of antipathy
> to the notion of keeping commandments
> should be entertained by any believer who is a
> serious student of the New Testament. Did not
> our Lord say, 'If you love me, you will keep my
> commandments' (John 14:15)?"[8]

The Biblical Commandments, such as you shall not kill, you shall not commit adultery, you shall not steal, all have to do with demonstrating love toward our neighbors. If we love our neighbors we will not covet from them, we will not kill

---

6   Octavius Winslow, "The Definition of Sanctification,"
    in *Sanctification*, Free Grace Broadcaster, Issue 215,
    Spring 2011, (Pensacola: Chapel Library, 2011), 6.
7   *Westminster Confession of Faith*, Chapter XIX, V.
8   Murray, 182.

them and we will not steal from them. And if we truly love God then we will certainly not have any gods before Him. We do things joyfully and freely for the sake of others once we are justified, not in order to become justified.

> "So far as this faith and riches must grow from day to day even unto the future life yet he remains in this mortal life on earth, and in this life he must needs govern his own body and have dealings with men. Here the works begin here a man cannot take his ease."[9]

This is motivated by a spirit of liberty. A Christian lives not in him- or herself, but in Christ and in their neighbor. We are free from sin and its consequences, but are bound to obedience through love. This means that we continue to follow the statutes of the Lord.

> "Why should I not therefore freely, joyfully, with all my heart, and with an eager will, do all things which I know are pleasing and acceptable to such a Father, Who has overwhelmed me with His inestimable riches? I will therefore give myself as a Christ to my neighbor, just as Christ offered Himself to me; I will do nothing in this life except what I see is necessary, profitable and salutary to my neighbor, since through faith, I have an abundance of all good things in Christ."[10]

9   Luther, 14.
10 Luther, 18.

When Jesus says, "If you love me you will obey my commandments" (John 14:15), He is not presenting something that is optional. The implication is that if there is no obedience to God's commandments by the believer there has been no forgiveness or recognition of God's love. A life of service to God and neighbor is the "natural" response to God's love and grace. Sanctification is growing in conformity to the spirituality of the divine law.[11] A hatred of sin will be part of the change to desire holiness in life. The sanctified one will find love for the law increasing, though the Christian is not under the law in terms of works righteousness, nor exposed to its curse.

One might respond by saying that love is enough by itself. If I love God and my neighbor, then I can freely do what I want.

> "Christian liberty is not the license to do as I want, but is rather being liberated to live within what God's law requires. The idea that love is its own law is a human mirage with no warrant in Scripture. Love alone does not tell me what I ought to want and to do in every kind of situation; it still needs instruction in righteousness of the sort the Bible gives."[12]

---

11 Winslow, 6.
12 Arthur Holmes, *Ethics* (Downers Grove, IL: InterVarsity Press, 1984), 13.

It needs the law to provide the direction for what love ought to do. Love is not autonomous, but is objectively revealed in God's precepts. John assures us that we can know that we know Him if we keep His commandments (1 John 2:3). Even the Jew understands that the "objective of Torah study, as stressed in Biblical writings, is to inspire the fear of the Lord and to cultivate the love of man."[13] Biblical law becomes renewed in the consciousness of the Christian, and the heart is renewed in seeking holiness and goodness. The Biblical law remains relevant for the Christian as a form of moral guidance and binding upon the conscience. It speaks to Christians about what loving actions look like. Psalm 1 begins,

> "How blessed is the man who does not walk in
> the counsel of the wicked, Nor stand in the
> path of sinners, Nor sit in the seat of scoffers!
> But his delight is in the law of the Lord, And in
> His law he meditates day and night."

The Christian should maintain a desire to be taught the way of God's statues and to meditate upon these precepts.

In 1520 Martin Luther wrote, "A Christian man is a perfectly free lord of all, subject to none. A Christian man is a perfectly dutiful servant of

---

13 Samuel Blumenfield, "Thou Shalt Teach," in *Great Jew-
    ish Ideas*, 134.

all, subject to all."[14] This is the "law of liberty"
(James 1:25, 2:12). Regarding this law of liberty
and differentiating it from the Old Testament
law, Phillip Ross writes,

> "James does not oppose freedom (or liberty)
> against law, but suggests that real freedom re-
> quires willing submission to God's law, and
> that real obedience to the law must be freely
> given. Upon conversion Christians should want
> to obey God's law, not because they must, but
> because they believe it to be the best option
> available. God's law provides the only real free-
> dom. And conversely, freedom in Christ brings
> with it the personal desire to obey God's law."[15]

In Matthew 5:48 we are told by Jesus to be
perfect as our heavenly father is perfect. Divine
holiness and perfection should drive human
morality and behavior. To deny the King's law is
to deny the King.

> "How blessed are those whose way is blameless,
> Who walk in the law of the Lord. How blessed
> are those who observe His testimonies, Who
> seek Him with all their heart. They also do no
> unrighteousness; They walk in His ways. Thou
> hast ordained Thy precepts, That we should
> keep them diligently. Oh that my ways may be
> established To keep Thy statutes" (Psalm 119:1-
> 5).

---

14 Martin Luther, 7.
15 Ross, 55.

The driving force of Biblical ethics is to become Christ-like and the law points one in that direction. Once there is a new heart inclined toward God and empowered by God's Spirit, there is the possibility of resisting evil and desiring to obey God's law.

> "Whichever bind us as creatures of God, made in his image, to think that anything less than perfection conformable to the Father's own could be the norm and the goal of the believer's ethic. It is precisely this that underlies the Sermon on the Mount, it is this that it inculcates, in this it finds its epitome. And that, in summary, is the ethic which our Lord's teaching exhibits."[16]

VIRTUE IS THE FRUIT OF THE SPIRIT

This regenerate heart is capable of loving God and of becoming more obedient to God. This is from a new motive, not as meritorious, but as a loving response to God. The Bible commands love for God with all the heart, soul, strength, and mind and to love one's fellow human. But we are incapable of doing so on our own efforts. When faith is placed in Christ and one is born anew and given a new heart, that heart is now inclined toward God. God also gives the believer the gift of the Holy Spirit, which leads a person towards obedience to God. God's

16 Murray, 180.

Spirit is now within the believer empowering and sanctifying him. This will also alter the disposition of the believer as the Holy Spirit works on the human heart producing good fruits, and the product of these fruits demonstrates the presence of the Spirit.

The Fruit of the Holy Spirit is a Biblical concept summarized by the nine general attributes of a true Christian life according to Galatians 5:22-23 which says,

> "But the fruit of the Spirit is love, joy, peace, patience, kindness, goodness, faithfulness, gentleness, self-control; against such things there is no law."

The fruits of the Spirit are the God-produced virtues that are to be cherished and cultivated. Christian living is more than just ceasing to do evil, it is learning to do the good. This fruit should be the spiritual consequence of repentance and faith in Christ. These virtues are not natural to fallen humans but are produced by the agency of the Holy Spirit. They are the "supernatural" result of the Spirit's operations on the human heart. The change of heart and the presence of God's sanctifying Spirit produces a disposition to do good to others. It is represented in this passage as the heart yielding either good or bad fruit according to the nature of the tree. Bad seed produces a bad tree, yielding all manner of rotten fruit. Good seed produces a good tree and brings forth the beneficial fruit listed here. The tree of the Spirit produces good fruits, and the production of these fruit demonstrates the presence of the Spirit. Dependence upon God produces these consequences. As such, then, Christian character is not mere moral or legal correctness, but the possession of these virtues. This character change is possible and is due to the believer's union with Christ through His Spirit.

We glorify God by our fruitfulness. John 15:8 states that the Father is glorified by the bearing of much fruit. Fruitfulness honors him.

> "We must not be like the fig tree in the gospel, which had nothing but leaves … that is continually either mellowing or blossoming, and is ever without fruit. It is not profession but fruit that glorifies God."[17]

Trees in the garden are to be fruitful. We must bring forth the fruit of good character. It vindicates our faith. The Spirit is given to refashion the image of God in humans.

As one depends on God and learns to live a prayerful life of trust, God's Spirit will reproduce the life of Christ from the inside out, but this life will always be in conformity to God's law, and the law remains as a standard-bearer for moral

---

17 Thomas Watson, "Man's Chief End is to Glorify God," http://www.puritansermons.com/watson/watson5.htm, 6.

guidance and direction. The internal work of the Spirit producing virtuous fruit and the external guidance of the law will never come into conflict with one another.

These two sayings, therefore, are true:

"'Good works do not make a good man, but a good man does good works; evil works do not make a wicked man, but a wicked man does evil works;' so that it is always necessary that the 'substance' or person itself be good before there can be any good works, and that good works follow and proceed from the good person, as Christ also says, 'A corrupt tree does not bring forth good fruit, a good tree does not bring forth evil fruit.' It is clear that the fruits do not bear the tree, nor does the tree grow on the fruits, but, on the contrary, the trees bear the fruits and the fruits grow on the trees. As it is necessary, therefore, that the trees must exist before their fruits, and the fruits do not make trees either good or corrupt, but rather as the trees are so are the fruits they bear; so the person of a man must needs first be good or wicked before he does a good or a wicked work, and his works do not make him good or wicked, but he himself makes his works either good or wicked."[18]

There is no conflict between law-keeping and the fruit of the Spirit. Works can never make

---

18 Luther 15.

a human righteous, but one's works demonstrate the righteousness that has already been given in Christ. It is true, by their fruits a person is known. "Although the Christian is thus free from all works, he ought in this liberty to empty himself, to take upon himself the form of a servant."[19] Law and love should be seen as complimentary to one another and not as contradictory. All acceptable duties flow naturally from one's love for God.

Sanctification, the ongoing life of holiness, is demonstrated by obedience to the law. In Christ, with a new heart and the presence of the Holy Spirit within, there is now the power to do the good and to live righteously (Jeremiah 31:31-34, Hebrews 8:8-12). This is the natural fruit of the changed life. By understanding the grace of God and relying on God's Spirit that comes into the life of the person who places faith in Christ, the person becomes capable of obeying God's law, though never perfectly, until glorification when one is fully restored in the presence of God in the afterlife. The Christian, however, should be progressively growing in obedience and righteousness by trusting God and depending on the Holy Spirit, given when rebirth occurs. The Spirit duplicates the moral life of Christ in the believer

---

19 Luther 17.

producing the Christian virtues called the Fruit of the Spirit.

7. Ends Must Also Be Considered

A life is greatly affected by the ends it seeks. The purpose of life is linked to ethics because that which we live for frequently becomes the reason we cling to the values we hold or why we act like we do. There are a variety of possible ends that people can pursue in life and most of these ends are self-directed and are sought to achieve one's own personal sense of happiness. These could include such ends as pleasure, wealth, fame, prestige, etc. The ancient philosopher Aristotle observes that all human ends are ultimately for the purpose of achieving the only final and complete end; this natural end for humans is happiness. He writes, "Happiness, then, is apparently something complete and self-sufficient, since it is the end of the things achievable in action."[1] Modern ethical

---

1 Aristotle, *The Nichomachean Ethics*, (Indianapolis: Hackett Publishing Company, 1999) 8.

thought is greatly influenced by Utilitarianism, which teaches that the good action is one which creates the greatest good or greatest happiness for the greatest number, including the self, though not giving priority to the self. These theories make the ends or consequences primary, and these ends are human-centered.

In contrast, the Christian teleology or reason for living is quite different. Paul says in 1 Corinthians 10:31 that whatever a person does, whether it be eating or drinking, it should all be done for the glory of God. We are to live not for ourselves but for honoring God. The *Westminster Shorter Catechism* states, "Man's chief end is to glorify God, and to enjoy Him forever."[2] To glorify God should be the ultimate end. The good life ought not to be the happy life, as Aristotle argues, or the life of pleasure, but rather the righteous life lived in obedience to God for the glory of God.

> "In their goodness all created things naturally tend towards God from whom they came …. Now natural things tend towards God, first, in that they declare God's glory, Psalm 19; second, in that they give occasion for us both to know and seek God, Romans 1:20; Acts 17:27; and third, in that they sustain our life that we may

---

2 *Westminster Shorter Catechism*, Question 1.

live to God, 1 Corinthians 10:31; 1 Timothy 4:3."[3]

Everything whether natural or artificial works toward some end; now, humans being rational creatures, must propose some end for themselves, and that should be, that they may lift up God in the world.[4]

Since God is the maker (Psalm 100:3) and sustainer (Colossians 1:16-17) of all that exists, then every human's end should be to glorify God. Proverbs 16:4 asserts, "The Lord has made everything for its own purpose" and that purpose is for His glory; this includes humankind. To glorify God is to rightly adore and honor God, for He will not share His deserved glory with anyone or anything else.

> "When we prefer God's glory above all other things; above credit, estate, relations, when the glory of God comes in competition with them, we prefer his glory before them."[5]

We glorify God by living completely for God. 2 Corinthians 5:15 adds, "And He died for all, that they who live should no longer live for themselves, but for Him who died and rose again on their behalf." All we have is through His free grace. Romans 14:7-8 continues,

3   Ames,102.
4   Watson, 1.
5   Watson, 5.

> "For not one of us lives for himself, and not one
> dies for himself; for if we live, we live for the
> Lord, or if we die, we die for the Lord; there-
> fore whether we live or die, we are the Lord's."

By this is God glorified: by our total dependence upon Him. One person lives for his money, another one lives to his belly and its pleasure. The design of a sinner's life is to gratify lust, but we glorify God when we live for God.[6] We glorify God when we honor God through all we are, all we have, and all we do.

In a moral universe humans should desire to be holy. We also glorify God as we practice holiness because God is holy. Too often in our contemporary society the goal is to *feel* good, but for the Christian it is more important to *be* good in deed. Christ is the model for moral living, so our human end is to become Christ-like, to become conformed to the image of Christ in our hearts and in our lives. This is what brings honor and glory to God. This is what we are made for; we are not made for ourselves and our own ends. The irony is that this cannot happen by our own human efforts. Not until we surrender to God and His will can it occur. We are defined by what we love most. What we love most becomes the end for which we seek. If we love self more than anything else, then our ends will all be self-

---

6   Watson, 7.

ish. But if we love that which is eternal above all else, then life's strivings will never be in vain. Humans live their lives *Coram Deo*, meaning before the face of God, whether they admit it or not. It is impossible to remove ourselves from God's presence. As such, all that we think, do, and say has meaning when it is done before God for the glory of God. The effect is true holiness or conformity to the moral perfections of the deity.

> "Since the highest kind of life for a human be-
> ing is that which approaches most closely the
> living and life-giving God, the nature of theo-
> logical life is living to God."[7]

By seeking to glorify and enjoy God there is an eternal reward as well. The final end includes great reward, though the reward is not the solitary motivation. There is an intrinsic reward in this life resulting from walking in righteousness before God, and there is the eternal heavenly reward of glorifying and enjoying God forever.

---

7   Ames, 77.

8. Testing The Morality Of An Action

In the light of what has been previously said, what should be the process for determining the morality of an action? How should a Christian determine what is right and what is wrong? Christian ethics recognizes that by relative standards some actions are superior to others, but **by God's standards** no one inherently or naturally does the morally good. No fallen sinful human is capable of pleasing God by their actions. People must first come to Christ by faith, then from faith they are able to subsequently do good works, works that are good *by God's standards*. Romans 14:22-23 states,

> "The faith which you have, have as your own conviction before God. Happy is he who does not condemn himself in what he approves. But he who doubts is condemned if he eats, because his eating is not from faith; and whatever is not from faith is sin."

Therefore the first necessary criteria for evaluating the morality of an action is determining whether or not it is done from faith in God. "Without faith it is impossible to please God" (Hebrews 11:6). Only a regenerated heart can lovingly desire to obey God and His law. Luther adds,

> "A good or bad builder makes a bad or a good house …. The workman makes the work like himself. So it is also with the works of man: as the man is, whether believer or unbeliever, so also is his work—good, if it was done in faith; wicked, if it was done in unbelief."[1]

Once a person places faith in Christ and has a new heart willing to be obedient to God, further instruction is needed on how to make correct ethical decisions and to live a moral life.

What should a faithful Christian do when confronted with a difficult moral situation or choice? Guidance must begin by determining what the Bible (God's Special Revelation) says about my doing this. Has God spoken moral law commands that are specific and unqualified to either do or not do something, such as "do not worship idols" or "do not steal," or "honor your mother and father"? If so, then the decision is clear and simple, obey God's clear law-commands. Though God has unmistakably spoken

---

1   Luther, 15.

and provided many detailed statements of truth, the Bible is not exhaustive truth. God's Word has not given concrete rules or laws to rule every specific moral decision found in life and work. Nevertheless, He has not left us directionless; so further direction must be sought.

Though a specific topic may not be directly addressed in the Scriptures there may be general Biblical law commands that would be applicable. For example, the directives in Romans 13 to obey civil authority, or "Be angry but sin not" (Ephesians 4:26), are general statements that an individual could use for providing personal direction. Other popular discussion topics might include questions like: how many children should one family have? Is smoking marijuana permissible since it is not specifically addressed in Scripture? Or should I send my children to a public school or not?

Implicit in all of this is the necessity for each person to know the Bible for oneself. However, the mere fact that someone claims that a specific act is contrary to general Biblical commands, does not make it so. The person must demonstrate that this is true. A matter must be regarded as indifferent until proven to be sinful. In Colossians 2:20-23, Paul lays this out,

> "If you have died with Christ to the elementary principles of the world, why, as if you were liv-

ing in the world, do you submit yourself to de-
crees, such as, 'Do not handle, do not taste, do
not touch!' (which all refer to things destined to
perish with the using)—in accordance with the
commandments and teachings of men? These
are matters which have, to be sure, the appear-
ance of wisdom in self-made religion and self-
abasement and severe treatment of the body,
but are of no value against fleshly indulgence."

God looks on the heart, and so the motive for
an action also matters. It is inseparable from obedience. True Christian morality should include
doing the right action for the right reason. Does
the action glorify God? Can it be done to God's
glory? Can you do the action boldly before the
holy face of God? A morally correct action is one
that should be by faith in God, motivated by love
for God and one's fellow man, and based on
Christian hope (with an eternal end or purpose in
mind). The law is loving and gracious, but it
cannot be obeyed by a sinful heart. The person
with a right understanding of the nature of love
will respond with a right motive of love.

The Christian is obliged not only to avoid
forbidden things and the occasions of temptation
to sin, but also practices that offend a weaker
Christian brother or sister. This principle is laid
out in 1 Corinthians 8:1-13 where Paul is advis-
ing the church in Corinth about a moral question
they were facing. It seems that they were won-

dering if, as "free Christians," it was permissible for them to eat meat that was left over after being offered as a sacrifice to idols. After telling the Corinthians that there is only one God and that the idols were not real gods, he says beginning in verse 7,

> "However not all men have this knowledge; but some, being accustomed to the idol until now, eat food as if it were sacrificed to an idol; and their conscience being weak is defiled. But food will not commend us to God; we are neither the worse if we do not eat, nor the better if we do eat. But take care that this liberty of yours does not somehow become a stumbling block to the weak. For if someone sees you, who have knowledge, dining in an idol's temple, will not his conscience, if he is weak, be strengthened to eat things sacrificed to idols? For through your knowledge he who is weak is ruined, the brother for whose sake Christ died. And so, by sinning against the brethren and wounding their conscience when it is weak you sin against Christ. Therefore, if food causes my brother to stumble, I will never eat meat again, so that I will not cause my brother to stumble."

So out of the motive of love for my brother, I should withhold from doing an action that may not be immoral in itself, but because it could cause a Christian friend to fall or stumble I should withhold from doing the action. This is true Christian charity or morality in action.

So, even though an act is not a sin in itself, I need to ask whether it would lead me or tend to lead me into temptation and cause me to sin, or tempt someone else or lead them into sin. Does the action lead to evil consequences? Scripture teaches plainly that we must avoid occasions of temptation to sin (Matthew 5:29, 30). Keep in mind that this command is conditional. No universal rule can be made in this matter. What is a real temptation to one person may not be a temptation at all to another.

For example, for a Japanese person converted from heathenism to keep a small brass Buddha in his house would be to invite temptation to lapse into old pagan ways. But for a retired Christian missionary to keep the same kind of image as a curio would not be considered a temptation. Each person must judge for himself what constitutes a temptation to him—and for others. For a man having been an alcoholic to take a social drink of wine would be morally wrong for the reason that he would likely be tempted to overindulge or become drunk. Drunkenness is clearly forbidden in Scripture (Romans 13:13, 1 Corinthians 5:11, Galatians 5:19-21), and he would, in effect, be inviting temptation. We must flee temptation (1 Corinthians 6:18, 10:14; 1 Timothy 6:11; 2 Timothy 2:22), but what this specifically means in each circumstance is far more ambiguous. Evaluating the consequences is the only way to make this determination using one's sanctified conscience. Of course, there are those cases when one is not sure whether the Bible forbids the action in question, or whether it will lead into temptation or offend a brother, whether my doing this would cause offense to a weaker Christian or cause him to stumble. The Biblical answer is simple: When in doubt, don't do it.

9. Conclusion

In the nineteenth century Friedrich Nietzsche declared the death of God, and by doing so thought that God and all related values are no longer relevant. Unfortunately even Nietzsche would likely be surprised to see how seriously his ideas have been taken and how far Western society has drifted from God and traditional Christian morality. It is obvious that universal values have become practically obsolete, but one thing learned in the most basic ethics classes is that there is a distinct difference between what *is* and what *ought* to be. This book has been about what ought to be, and is thereby calling its readers to return to or discover those values historically rooted in Christianity and the God of the Bible.

The law of God is based upon and demonstrative of God's holy moral nature, and is the universal standard for individual, familial, church, and social ethics.

> "The law of God ought to guide all our deliberations, all our actions, all which takes place in

our homes, and all that transpires outside of our
homes. (It is) an infallible ethical blueprint that
ought to direct the individual, the parent, the
elder and the civil magistrate."[1]

God's standards for morality are universal. Unbelievers are to follow them in the best interests of
self, family, and society; even unbelievers will
benefit from them. Acute awareness of God's
principles should also drive people to faith in
Christ. For Christians, God's law-commands are
the standard for right living. Believers who are
delivered from the dominion of sin are not under
the law as a means of salvation or condemnation,
nor exposed to its curse. They are under grace,
completely justified by the free favor of God, and
live under its powerful influence. Nevertheless,
the law is to be their guiding light for moral
direction.

Deuteronomy 6:4-9 proclaims:

"Here, O Israel! The Lord is our God, the Lord
is one! And you shall love the Lord your God
with all your heart and with all your soul and
with all your might. *And these words, which I am
commanding you today, shall be on your heart; and
you shall teach them diligently to your sons and
shall talk of them when you sit in your house and
when you walk by the way and when you lie down
and when you rise up.* And you shall bind them

---

1   Einwechter, 43.

as a sign on your hand and they shall be as frontals on your forehead. And you shall write them on the doorposts of your house and on your gates."

The Ten Commandments, in combination with the command to love God with all of one's heart and one's neighbor as oneself and from that love to then be motivated to obey His Commandments, is the essence of Christian morality.

"The works themselves do not justify him before God, but he does the works out of spontaneous love in obedience to God, and considers nothing except the approval of God. ... He is obliged to teach them to his children and be occupied with them in all his activities, even while walking by the way, lying down, rising up. This is the human side of the covenant—total involvement and total responsibility. There is no part of man's existence that is unrelated to God as man obediently lives in accord with the requirements of the covenant."[2]

In this our lives are to be like Jesus, lives lived in righteous obedience to God and motivated by a genuine love for the God of mercy. Not only are we to obey God's law as exemplified by Jesus but we are to love *as He loved*. This is what it means to be conformed to the image of Christ and to be like Jesus.

---

2 Silberman, 157-158.

In the book *Screwtape Letters*, C. S. Lewis creates a series of letters from a character named Screwtape, a head demon in hell, to his apprentice nephew, Wormwood, who is a disciple of Screwtape and is attempting to corrupt a human living on earth. Screwtape consistently sends Wormwood letters about how he can manipulate and corrupt targeted human beings. Finally Screwtape says of God, whom he refers to in the third person and as the enemy:

> "Now it may surprise you to learn that in his efforts to get permanent possession of a soul, He relies on the troughs more than the peaks; some of his special favourites have gone through longer and deeper troughs than anyone else. The reason is this. To us a human is primarily food; our aim is the absorption of its will into ours, the increase of our own area of selfhood at its expense. But the obedience which the Enemy demands of men is quite a different thing. One must face the fact that all the talk about His love for men, and His service being perfect freedom is not (as one would gladly believe) mere propaganda, but an appalling truth. He really does want to fill the universe with a lot of loathsome little replicas of Himself—creatures whose life, on its miniature scale, will be qualitatively like His own, not because He has absorbed them but because their wills freely conform to His. We want cattle who can finally become food; He wants ser-

vants who can finally become sons. We want to suck in, He wants to give out. We are empty and would be filled; He is full and flows over. Our war aim is a world in which Our Father Below has drawn all other beings into himself: the Enemy wants a world full of beings united to Him but still distinct."[3]

Thus the highest and best kind of life for a human being is one which approaches most closely the living and life-giving God.[4] Therefore, for any action to be a truly moral good,

"it must be done from a right principle, performed by a right rule, and intended for a right end. It must be done from a right principle: this is the love of God …. It must be performed by a right rule: this is the revealed will of God …. The moral law … is the rule of our obedience. It is a complete system of duty; considered as moral, it is immutably the rule of our conduct. It must be intended for a right end: this is the glory of the Supreme Being."[5]

---

3   C. S. Lewis, *Screwtape Letters*, (New York: HarperCollins Publishers,1996) 38-39.

4   Ames, 77.

5   Booth, "The Motive of Sanctification," in *Sanctification*, Free Grace Broadcaster Issue 215, Spring 2011 (Pensacola: Chapel Library, 2011), 30.

Epilogue

This book is about ethics and how humans created in the image of God are supposed to live. The morality established by God is primarily found in His law which defines God's covenantal relationship to humans. When God created us He established a means whereby we should relate to Him and that is on the basis of covenant. A covenant is an established lawful contract or bond that institutes the legal relationship between two persons, generally including various stipulations to maintain the contractual agreement. Throughout Scripture God relates to humans on the basis of covenant, so that all humans are either in a good familial, covenantal relationship with God due to their obedience to God's commands, or an antagonistic relationship due to their covenant-breaking.

Scriptural law establishes the criteria by which humans can maintain a righteous relationship with God, complete perfect obedience to God's moral law. But, as has been clearly laid out in this book, all humans repeatedly break God's lawful, moral commands, break covenant with God, and thus stand under God's wrath and condemnation. It is a desperate situation deserving of our death. The only way to recover a right-standing with God and to inherit eternal life is by affirming God's grace in His atonement or sacrifice offered through Jesus Christ for our disobedient lawlessness. Jesus, the only righteous God/man lived a life of complete obedience to the Father; thus He was not deserving of death. His selfless death can therefore pay for our sins.

John 1:12 says, "But as many as received Him, to them He gave the right to be children of God, even to those who believe in His name." So in spite of our sins, if we seek out forgiveness through Christ and place faith in Jesus, we can find justification or a restored right covenantal connection to God giving us access to a deep personal relationship with God the Father.

> "If you confess with your mouth that Jesus is Lord and believe in your heart that God has raised Him from the dead you will be saved" (Romans 10:9).

When a person places their faith in Jesus and understands the greatness of this love, then obedience to God's commands becomes the basis for living the good life. Biblical ethics is about obeying God's commands from the motive of love and giving God the glory He deserves. This will necessarily lead to fruitful moral living.

PILGRIM PLATFORM BOOKS BY PHILLIP A. ROSS

The Work At Zion—A Reckoning, Two-volume set, 1996.

Practically Christian—Applying James Today, 2006.

The Wisdom of Jesus Christ in the Book of Proverbs, 2006.

Marking God's Word—Understanding Jesus, 2006.

Acts of Faith—Kingdom Advancement, 2007.

Informal Christianity—Refining Christ's Church, 2007.

Engagement—Establishing Relationship in Christ, 1996, 2008.

It's About Time!—The Time Is Now, 2008.

The Big Ten—A Study of the Ten Commandments, 2001, 2008.

Arsy Varsy—Reclaiming The Gospel in First Corinthians, 2008.

Varsy Arsy—Proclaiming The Gospel in Second Corinthians, 2009.

Colossians—Christos Singularis, 2010.

Rock Mountain Creed—The Sermon on the Mount, 2011.

The True Mystery of the Mystical Presence, 2011.

Peter's Vision of Christ's Purpose in First Peter, 2011.

Peter's Vision of The End in Second Peter, 2012.

The Religious History of Nineteenth Century Marietta, Thomas Jefferson Summers, 1903, 2012 (editor).

Conflict of Ages—The Great Debate of the Moral Relations of God and Man, Edward Beecher, 1853, 2012 (editor).

Concord Of Ages—The Individual And Organic Harmony Of God And Man, Edward Beecher, D. D., 1859, 2013 (editor).

Ephesians—Recovering the Vision of a Sustainable Church in Christ, 2014.

Available on www.pilgrim-platform.org/books or Amazon.com.